PERFECT PARTIES

PERFECT PARTIES

Tips and Advice from a New York Party Planner

LINNEA JOHANSSON

Foreword by Marcus Samuelsson
Edited by Robert Andersson   Photographs by Paul Brissman

Skyhorse Publishing

www.skyhorsepublishing.com

10 9 8 7 6 5 4 3 2 1

Library of Congress Cataloging-in-Publication Data

Johansson, Linnea.
   Perfect parties : tips and advice from a new york party planner / Linnea Johansson Robert
Andersson ; Photographs by Paul Brissman.
      p. cm.
   ISBN 978-1-60239-116-1 (hardcover : alk. paper)
   1. Entertaining. 2. Cookery. 3. Menus. I. Andersson, Robert. II. Brissman, Paul. III. Title.

TX731.J58 2007
641.5—dc22
                              2007018503

Printed in China

PERFECT PARTIES

Party Memories

Networking

Flower Mar

NYC

Planning

Dinner

Mingling

Buffet

Napkin Folds

Flower Arrangement

Cocktail Party

Contents:

For The Bar

Brunch

Hors D'oeuvres

Bubbly

FOREWORD

INVITING PEOPLE INTO your home for a party is an intimate gesture. Suddenly you're exposed: everything from your cooking to your wallpaper is out in the open, and you immediately begin to worry if people are going to have fun, whether they'll like the soup, or whether they'll ask for vodka when you only have wine. Suddenly the decision to throw a party has become a stressor when it should be a joy.

But the people you've invited haven't come to critique you; they've come to learn more about you. So throwing a great party is really just a matter of demonstrating a little about who you are through the food, drinks, decoration, and music you select.

For me, in the restaurant world, every event is about proper planning. But for a party in your home, the key is to both plan well and to allow for a little improvisation. That's when the magic happens. People today don't expect to sit down and be served. People want to participate. When my grandmother threw a party, she worked in the kitchen all evening and sat down with her guests only over coffee. People get very uncomfortable that way today. A party where the host or hostess mingles and introduces people and is full of energy is more interesting and more fun for everyone.

What you can do ahead of time is decide the theme of your party, pick your decorations, buy your bar supplies and wine, and prepare certain foods before people arrive. It's important that as you create your menu, you keep your schedule in mind. Don't decide on three courses that all need to be served piping hot. Food that's best at room temperature can be prepared ahead of time. Everyone loves easy-to-handle "finger" food. Leave yourself only one dish that needs to be served fresh and hot. It's less work for you and more fun for everyone else.

The same concept can work for drinks. In most situations, it's perfectly fine to put out bottles and mixers and let guests serve themselves. As an alternative, you can have one blended specialty drink like sangria or margaritas made up ahead of time so no one is weighed down by bartending duties.

In short, we are as different as the parties we throw, and what I love about *Perfect Parties* is that it gives you such a variety, and offers them in a dazzling display of visual creativity. Linnea covers everything from recipes to themes to flowers to place settings. She even touches on clothing to wear at your parties. Throwing a party is a way to express yourself; Linnea's gift to her readers is that she can inspire you with possibilities.

Everything in this book is based on classic party ideas. But Linnea adds her own creative twists which will wow your guests without overwhelming them. She makes hamburgers out of foie gras. They come with French fries, too, served with wasabi mustard and curry ketchup. She bakes cupcakes for dessert but adds chocolate truffles. She recommends mixed fruit for brunch, but grilled and on a skewer. With Linnea, tired ideas become new again, so you can still have your traditional brunch or barbeque, infused with imagination and flair.

Linnea and I have been working (and partying) in New York for many years. It is a wonderful place because there are so many different people from so many different cultures. You'll never be short on good party ideas here. But the biggest challenge for a New Yorker planning a party at home is that space is limited, especially kitchen space. Don't let that prevent you from throwing a great party. Linnea has some great ideas on how to work with what you have.

Perfect Parties is a wonderful book that can add some celebrity glamour to your everyday life. Linnea has been inspired by her many famous clients over the years. Now, it's her turn to inspire you. Read this book, and get ready to throw a perfect party.

> – Marcus Samuelsson
> Executive Chef
> Aquavit Restaurant

PLANNING

Turning Central Park Zoo into a lavish party venue was hands down one of the most challenging tasks I have worked on as an event planer. Four thousand guests were invited and the event required a year of planning. The penguin house was turned into a caviar bar, the polar bear area into a sushi station; an opera singer accompanied the sea lions on top of their cave, and in the midst of everything dancers and circus artists performed amongst the guests. More than a thousand colorful silk pillows had been especially designed for the party and overflowed the park's benches. Pink Chinese lanterns dangled from the trees and several thousand candles were spread out on the grounds. Exotic drinks were served from bamboo huts, and while waiting for the restrooms, guests could swing in swings. It was like stepping into a fairytale or a Tim Burton movie. Parties of this magnitude give even the most experienced event planner night sweats. There is always something that can go awry and put a damper on the magical atmosphere. This time the monkeys were convinced they sang better then the opera singer on the cliff next to them, and all of a sudden a rotten scent spread in the penguin house where the guests indulged in caviar and oysters. Many of them couldn't continue eating. Despite this, the party was a success, and was nominated as one of the best that year.

CREATIVE PLANNING

WHETHER *it's three or three thousand people on your guest list, the procedure is the same when planning your party. Always start with creative planning, which will help you decide the concept and theme of your party. For example, what your décor is going to look like, what type of drinks you want to serve, and the elements that will make your bash unique. For a normal sized event, with 3–25 invited guests, four weeks before the event is a good time to sit down and start planning. If the party is a bigger size, you will most probably need to start your creative planning a bit earlier to allow more time to execute your ideas. Your goal should always be to make your party a haven for yourself and your guests, where for a few hours you can hang out and experience something out of the ordinary together. Sound difficult? It's not. Every time you want to throw a party, just ask yourself the same eight simple questions. You will be amazed how quickly they provide you with a different concept each time you want to have a ball.*

Start with the most important question:

1. WHY THROW A PARTY?

You got a new job and want to get to know your co-workers better. You recently started your own business and wouldn't mind a write up in the local paper. You want to surprise your best friend, who finally just got her scuba diving certificate. The very reason why you are throwing a party decides how you will shape it. Events where you have a specific goal, like getting publicity or raising money for a cause differ from parties thrown with friends and acquaintances just for the fun of it. Mainly the guest list is what will differ (see p. 14).

This book mostly focuses on private parties for friends and family.

Don't be bashful.

Bored? Don't sit around and wait until someone gets a year older or hitched. Look around and you will find tons of reasons to throw a party to make your everyday life a little bit more glamorous, a little bit more often.

– Get your Oprah on for a night and invite your friends, and their favorite paperbacks, to a book-swapping party.
– Spring has arrived. Buy flowerpots, dirt, and seeds. Pre-cultivating-party! (Spring officially starts close to March 21each year.)
–Your favorite band has a new CD out. Release party at your house, where you all review their new songs. (The worst critic gets no cake.)
– It's February. You are on the east coast, and it's cold and dark. Cheer up! It's also the very same month as the Carnival in Rio kicks off. Play samba music, pass around spicy hors d'oeuvres and serve papaya-tinis to kick up the heat.
– You have subscribed to a food magazine for over a year now. Don't you want to try your new impressive culinary skills on your closest friends? Invite them to a three-course dinner.
– It's fall, and your front yard is a mess. Invite your friends and serve them a drink when they arrive. Then swap some apple picking and leaf raking chores for a great brunch.

Shopoholic? Then you'll like planning parties. Look forward to fun and creative conversations with experts in their fields while looking for everything from fabrics to tea for your event.

Party for PR

In cities like New York City and Los Angeles, organizations and companies often throw extraordinary parties to get valuable media exposure. One million dollars for a PR event like this is not an unusual budget. Do you run your own company, or are you devoted to a nonprofit organization, and could really use some press coverage of your own? Invite local dailies, radio stations, web editors, and your local TV station to a press breakfast, tea party, or whatever kind of function you find suitable. At the gathering you'll have a great opportunity to talk about your business or organization, and the press will be able to ask questions. Always have a theme for an event like this and announce it on the invitation. For example, fall's new flower trends will be shown and explained in your flower shop, or a club's new soccer coach will be introduced. Keep the gathering short and preferably on a Monday to Friday before lunch. This way the journalists get as much time as possible to meet their deadlines. The event should be held in a public space, not in your own private home, and explain to friends and family that this is a business event – and sorry, no invite for your Aunt Sarah!

2. WHAT TYPE OF PARTY?

An intimate three-course dinner in your kitchen for your new co-workers? A PR party, with a doggy fashion show promoting your new company that designs pets-wear? A surprise pool party for your friend with the new scuba diving certificate? The options are endless, but keep in mind not to make your party more crazy and ambitious than your schedule allows. It should be a joy to plan, not another stressful task on your already packed "to-do" list. Remember, there are always fabulous short cuts you can use. Having difficulties fitting in that three-course dinner for your co-workers between work, yoga, your appointment at the DMV, and your weekly pottery class? Rethink, but don't drop, your original idea to have a ball! Buy marshmallows, graham crackers, and chocolate bars at the gas station next time you pump, and greet your guests to a s'mores BBQ. Pair the s'mores with lots of champagne for a dash of class.

3. GUESTS?

Your guest list will vary depending on your two previous answers: Why are you having a party? What type of party are you throwing? Decide at an early stage how many guests you want to invite so you can plan the party's budget, pick a venue, and decide what food and drink to serve. Always mix old and new faces to achieve a dynamic and fun event. A smaller party's guest list requires more time and thought compared to bigger affairs to achieve the right mix of guests. At a press or charity event, you need to stay focused on the party's purpose and ban friends and family altogether at the press party.

At the charity function, they might be more suitable—especially if they have a little extra cash.

4. TIMING?

Be open-minded. A party doesn't have to be at night. It's as fabulous to meet up in the middle of the day as after dark. What hour your event starts affects the type of food you are expected to serve. If you don't have the time or budget to cook lots of food, it's perfect to throw a late cocktail party. Guests will have eaten before they arrive, and you can simply serve canapés that look luxurious but are simple to make and friendly to your wallet. To avoid awkward misunderstandings and starving guests, give a hint on the invitation to what will be served. For example, Canapé & Cocktails, Dessert Buffet, Wine Tasting.

5. BUDGET?

It's easy to get a little bit too inspired, or all of a sudden fear that the guests will be disappointed if you don't treat them to at least three different types of wine during dinner. But you won't enjoy having mac and cheese for weeks to compensate for overspending on champagne and caviar. Therefore, make a budget before you proceed with your party plans. Write down the sum you want to spend, then add 10 percent as an emergency buffer for unexpected costs. There is no better way to keep a budget then to have plenty of time to call different stores and rentals to compare prices. For example, make as much of your own décor as possible. Do you love creating flower arrangements? If so, use most of the décor budget on greens. Are you an amazing cook? Spend most of your money on food, and so on. If you are a notorious overspender, withdraw your budgeted amount and keep the money in an envelope, paying all your expenses in cash. When the envelope is empty you're done shopping, even if things are missing. That's the law! (Hint: always start with the most important things first.)

6. VENUE?

A big chunk of how much time and effort you have to put into your party preparations depends on the venue you pick. There are three different types of locations: your home, a restaurant/catering hall, and raw-venues. They all have their pros and cons. Restaurants are practical but because of other possible guests, sometimes that intimate and vibrating party atmosphere disappears, and restaurants can easily become pricey. Raw-venues are even more expensive since you have to arrange everything from furniture and decorations, to lighting and food. This means you also have to put in a lot of time and planning. But it also lets you create exactly the atmosphere you want. Outdoors is another type of raw-venue, which can be amazing if the weather is great. If it's poor, you're stuck. Actually the saying "home, sweet home" goes for parties most of the time as well. There's no rental fee, you can fit more guests than you think, the furniture and kitchen is in place, and you can easily create a new mood with the right lighting and decorations.

7. FOOD AND BEVERAGE?

Consider your previous answers before you decide what you want to treat your guests to. What type of party is it, what time during the day or evening will it kick off, how are the circumstances for preparing the food at the venue, how many guests, and so on. Also remember not to get an anxiety attack when planning the food. Make simple dishes, and prepare as much as possible in advance. This way you can mingle more with your guests and not be chained to the stove the whole evening.

8. YOUR TWIST?

What makes a party go from fine to sensationally extraordinary? The answer is: a theme. With the same drinks, guest list, and budget a theme will help you create an experience so different that your guests will talk about it for weeks after. The theme can be something as simple as a color theme, or more advanced like a full transformation of your apartment into a Caribbean cruise—merengue tunes, a tropical buffet in the kitchen, and a cabana in the living room where the guests sip pina coladas while competing in shuffleboard. A theme not only adds a twist that makes your party special, it also helps you plan by giving you inspiration, guidelines, and ideas. No matter what your theme is, it should always be reflected in everything you do, from the design to the dessert.

What to Eat When?

If your ambition is to be a perfect party host, certain foods should be served at certain hours. So memorize the information below. On the other hand, if you break these old rules no one will ever object. The chart's time interval indicates between which hours the party should start:

9–11 AM: Breakfast

11 AM–1 PM: Lunch/Brunch

2–4 PM: Tea party

5–9 PM: Cocktail party

6–9 PM: Dinner/Buffet

Create decorations that enhance your party's theme and mood.

FAVORITE PARTY THEMES

❧ AUCTION HOUSE

Decorate your living room with inexpensive Andy Warhol posters, or works from another artist. Print up works from the artist, and tape them around regular water glasses. Place tealights in the glasses and voila! New candleholders! White plates are easily transformed into matching party trays by printing the artist's work onto overhead plastic sheets that you attach with double-stick tape. Conduct a silent auction for the posters where the guests write their bids on paper scraps. Donate the money raised to charity, or a project you are all passionate about. Just let your friends know where the money will end up before you start the bidding.

❧ ROLLER GIRLS

Bring a boom box to your nearest club, or borrow your local high school's gym. Play the Bee Gees, and get those wheels going! Write on the invitation that you want to see your guests in knee-high socks, eye-catching colorful 70s shorts, and old-fashioned roller skates, but they should leave the rollerblades at home. Pass around neon sweatbands to guests rolling through the door and treat them to champagne and burgers. Helmets are strongly recommended.

❧ SPA GETAWAY

Play relaxing tunes, and sip super-healthy smoothies with seaweed, wheat grass, or algae. The ickier it sounds, the more Hollywood it probably is. Spread out comfy pillows, and light up all those old aroma therapy candles you have. Apply facials and do each other's nails.

❧ LEARN SOMETHING NEW

Karate, high diving, wine tasting, or lace making? No matter what kind of hobby you've dreamt of trying the past years, chances are your friends want to try it as well. Find an instructor, ask how much he or she charges, or use your charm to get a session for free—after all, if you guys like it, you are potential future clients. Send out invitations matching the adventure of the day and serve a buffet afterwards where you can talk about your brand-new hobby.

❧ THE SWEDISH FEST

Sweden has given us treats like the music group Abba, IKEA, tennis player Björn Borg, clothing giant H&M, and Volvo. Celebrate it on June 6, Sweden's national holiday. Find a meatball recipe online, drink "snaps" (small shots of pure spiced vodka), and sing karaoke to Swedish hits from Roxette, the Cardigans, and Ace of Base. Go outdoors to compete in traditional Swedish games by dividing your guests into two teams. See which group can throw a rubber boot the farthest, take turns running with a spoon in your mouths, and see who can balance a potato the quickest. Yes, Swedes really play these games.

❧ A NIGHT ON THE STRIP

Tempt your friends to a poker evening where you serve sumptuous sandwiches and other tasty late-night snacks. Gents are encouraged to dress like their favorite "rat pack" member (yes, this includes bow ties) and ladies can show up in their most bedazzling cocktail dresses. Play Elvis in the background and dig out your Christmas decorations early this year. A Vegas party can never be too kitsch!

❧ RED CARPET PREMIERE

Your favorite movie this year has just been released on DVD. Roll out your red rug and create your very own red carpet premiere. Take pictures of the arriving guests, preferably with the movie's poster in the background. If you are using a digital camera, make sure to email the pictures to your friends a few days after the event. With a Polaroid camera you can give away the pictures to the guests when they are leaving. After an hour's mingling with cocktails and canapés, it's time for the screening, complete with popcorn. If you want to end the party in grand style, surprise your guests with a huge limousine and take them to a nightclub to continue the fete.

PRACTICAL PLANNING

WHEN YOU'VE ANSWERED *all eight questions, you now have your unique party concept. You're done with the creative planning phase. Now it's time for the next step: practical planning. It's time to make all your great ideas a reality. Everything from making the invitations and sending them out on time, to calculating when to put the rice on the stove so it's ready at the same time as the chicken entree. The more exact you are with your planning, the smoother your party will run, and the more time you'll have for fun and to look gorgeous. Like creative planning, start with the practicals approximately four weeks before your event if it's a regular sized party. To make sure you don't forget anything use a "slacker's guide." (See p. 19)*

First aid for an event planner is a toolbox overflowing with gear such as staple and glue guns, tape measures, adhesive tape, Band-Aids, and other indispensable equipment.

Slacker's Party Guide

This slacker's guide is to help plan a regular party in your home. If it's a truly grand occasion, like a wedding or a family reunion, keep in mind that you need much more time than four weeks to prep for the occasion. A smaller gathering, with invites over the phone, requires shorter time. Use the guide as a model and mold it to fit your specific needs. Finish your creative planning before using it though, so you know what kind of event you want to throw.

4 weeks before

- Decide on a theme.
- Measure the space where your event will be held.
- Draw a floor plan and make sure all your party décor fits.
- Design the invitations.
- Create a budget.

3 weeks before

- Send out the invitations.
- Decide on menu and beverages.
- Make a shopping list with approximated costs and compare it with your budget.

2 weeks before

- Plan the décor in detail and where you can find needed materials.
- Approximate your décor costs. Compare with budget.

1 week before

- Verify your RSVP list. Call or send emails to guests you haven't heard from.
- Buy beverages and decorations, except flowers and other perishables.
- Call your florist. Make sure what you need is in stock or can be ordered.
- Borrow or rent extra equipment like chairs, tables, and china if needed.

2 days before

- Make a service schedule. Write down your exact plan for the event and be as precise as possible. For example, which food and drinks are you going to serve, and at what hour? The schedule will help you find things you might have forgotten about and make your party run smoothly.
- Purchase the food.
- Double-check your shopping lists and make sure that you have everything you need.
- Decide what to wear to avoid last minute fashion stress.

The day before

- If you are having a seated dinner, make your seating arrangements. Don't make it sooner since last minute changes and cancellations are common.
- Pick up the flowers if you are designing flower arrangements.
- Prepare all décor, except flower arrangements.
- Set the tables and make sure everything fits and looks great.
- Set up possible bar locations.
- Prepare as much of the food as possible.

The day of the party!

- Create the flower arrangements in the morning.
- Buy ice.
- Get some good music going and cook the rest of your food.
- Chill the bottled beverages that are supposed to be served cold. It takes about 30 minutes for a 25 oz. bottle of wine to cool down in an ice bath.
- Get dressed and have all preparations done except last minute food one hour prior to your party. Make all final preparations, sip on a yummy drink, and double-check everything.
- Welcome your guests!

Budget Tips

Having trouble making ends meet with the budget? Here are some great cost-cutting ideas:

- At a larger event, the best way to save money is to cut down on the alcohol. Don't bother with a full bar, simply serve a few of your favorite cocktails mixed in bulk.
- To cut costs at a smaller gathering where you plan to serve a full meal, such as a dinner or buffet, decrease the number of guests invited.
- Can't afford dinner? Have a function where you just serve dessert and cocktails.
- Share the honor, responsibilities, and the budget for a party with one or two friends.
- You want to invite lots of guests, but economize on food expenses? Send out two different invitations. One dinner invite for a few selected guests, and a larger invite list for a cocktail gathering, starting when the dinner is ended.

Save Halloween

It's a fact: traditional parties like Halloween and the 4th of July occur each year. To save cash, plan them one year ahead and bargain-hunt table cloths, china, hats, and other accessories for half the price, just when the current season is over. Store and bring out next time it's trick or treat.

Balance Your Budget

Divide your budget into separate expense groups, and write down you different costs under each suitable group. When done, add all your cos together and there it is: your budget.

Invitations: Cards, envelopes, pencils, and other supplies needed for your invitations. Don't forget to include postage.

Food: Everything edible that is served at the party.

Beverages: Everything drinkable at the bash, and everything you need when garnishing the cocktails (for example, lime wedges and straws).

Décor: Candles, flowers, light bulbs, table cloths, table seating cards, napkin rings purchased for the occasion, fabrics, napkins — in short, everything to decorate your bash.

Entertainment: Music, the fee for your favorite local rock band or a belly dancer, the DVD for movie night, games for board game night, rented speakers, and so on.

Other Expenses: Possible venue fees, rented china, glasses, tables and chairs, wait staff, photographer, limousine, cleaning products, extra toiletries, and other costs that pop up and don't fit under any of the other expense posts.

10 percent Buffer: Add up the costs, and calculate ten percent of that sum. Add the ten percent to your budget and use it as your buffer for unexpected last minute expenses.

Planning is key to a successful party. Get a big folder out, and start collecting all your information and facts for the event; the budget, telephone numbers, sketches of your decorations, ideas for the menus, and shopping lists.

GUESTS

As an event planner you meet lots of celebrities, and during the years I've learned that they all have different requirements. Donald Trump doesn't drink alcohol, but loves meatballs. Nelson Mandela likes spicy food, while Salma Hayek detests curry. Some encounters have been more pleasant than others. At one of my parties I bumped into Woody Allen so hard that he ended up crumpled on the floor, and at a fashion event I lost my assistant when Justin Timberlake hired him as his new background dancer on the spot.

It's crucial to get interesting guests to your galas since companies spend lots of money on their events—sometimes millions of dollars. In return, they want to be seen in magazines and TV, to strengthen their brand, and nothing boosts publicity like a star-studded event.

Well-known faces get several party invitations a day, so in order to get their attention you need to create an invitation that stands out. Gift bags never hurt either. Once I sent out one pearl earring as part of the invitation; it's match was given to the guests when they arrived at the party. I've delivered flowers with invitations in the bouquets, praline boxes with party essentials written on the bonbons, and I've sent people off to the tailor where they got their measurements taken and at the event they found out where they could pick up their free custom-made shirt a couple of weeks later. The most expensive gift bag I've ever handed out was a specialty designed Burberry bag with a tiger pattern fabric. It contained luxurious skin and hair care products worth tens of thousands of dollars.

MIX IT UP

YOU CAN COOK *a buffet with the most sensational of flavors and transform your living room into a lavish Greek temple, but no matter what, it is still the guests and the energy they bring that will make your party a success in the end. The golden rule is to always invite a good mix of old and new faces. Although it may feel a bit uncomfortable to approach and invite people you aren't tight with, find the courage. Who wouldn't appreciate an invitation to a party? A mix of old or new friends will make your party more dynamic and create new friendships, interesting conversations, and great networking opportunities throughout the night for your guests. A party where everyone already knows each other becomes routine, but of course there are exceptions. At the bridal shower for the bride-to-be, where you celebrate that one of your closest friends is marrying, you only invite familiar faces.*

Party Memories

Put a guest book on the table and ask your friends to write something about the occasion; it will become an elegant and fun memento. Keep a disposable or Polaroid camera next to the book so the guests can take pictures. Attach the pictures in the book or give them as gifts to your guests.

Q&A About Guests

What should I do if someone calls last minute and asks to bring along some extra guests?

You're familiar with the saying "The more the merrier." Most of the time that absolutely goes when having a party, but it's also OK to say no. A seated dinner with extra guests might, for example, require major rearrangements and you would have to dig deeper in your wallet to buy more food. An option to avoid stressful last-minute changes is to invite the extra guests to join you for dessert or after dinner coktails. Always have extra bread, cheese, snacks, and dip for your buffet or cocktail party. This way, you are prepared if some extra guests crash your bash, and keep in mind that most people prefer to RSVP + 1.

Do I really have to invite all my relatives for important birthdays, baptisms, and weddings?

Not really, but think about it. You can easily hurt someone's feelings if you invite just a few of your relatives, even if you haven't seen the person you are leaving out for ages. And that's not cool.

Help, I invited too many guests. Can I pull back invitations that have already been sent out?

No, but you can save face gracefully if someone RSVPs last minute or after the set date. Tell them that you are sad to have to inform them that the respond has been greater than you expected, and that the guest list has already been filled up. If everyone RSVPs on time you have to bite the bullet.

What should I do if a guest doesn't follow the dress code that I wrote on the invitation?

Don't judge a book by its cover (especially not this one). If you really want everyone to follow a dress theme, a tip is to stack up with extra masks, flowers, or other suitable props. This way you are well prepared when guests show up that have skipped out on the dress code.

If I write an RSVP date on the invitation, can I expect everyone to reply, even the ones that can't attend?

Oh, yeah! If you have taken the time to invite someone, that person can take the time to get back to you—even if he or she can't make it. If you haven't heard from people a week before your party, you are entitled to call or email and ask if they have received the invitation, and if they plan to attend or not.

My feet hurt and it's getting late. How do I get my guests to leave?

Set up a small coffee bar for your late nighters. The same way coffee after a meal signals that the dinner is over, this gesture hints that the party soon will come to its end. If the coffee doesn't have the wanted effect, slowly turn down the music, and even discreetly switch on a few lights in the room. But don't start cleaning until all guests have left. A foolproof way to avoid lingering guests is to state the hours of your party on the invitation. This is especially recommended for daytime or early evening affairs.

THE INVITATION

ONCE YOU'VE SETTLED *on what old and new faces you want to see at your party, it's time to invite them. Put effort and thought into your invitation since it will be the guests' first impression of your affair. Let the invitation design reflect your party's theme and signal that something out of the ordinary is to be expected. Think of it as marketing.*

An eye-catching invitation is the best way to ensure attendance of a stellar crowd. Today you can find free invitation services online (see p. 31). It's an inexpensive and quick way to send out your invitations. It is also convenient for you and your guests to RSVP via email. You can easily tally up how many guests have agreed to attend. An extra treat is that the guests can keep in touch online, and you can send out reminders easily. On the other hand, nothing creates bigger expectations for the occasion and gives a more glamourous impression than a traditional paper invitation. Reflect on how important the invitation is for the party you are having and decide how much time and money you are prepared to spend on it. If you plan on celebrating the season premiere of your favorite TV series, maybe an email with a retouched picture of you, posing with your favorite star, is enough. (Ask a technically inclined friend if you need help with the retouching.) For

a twentieth anniversary or other grand affairs, a paper invitation is more suitable. It's a jubilee, and it gives a more serious impression for guests that might have to travel for the occasion. A third alternative is to call and invite your guests over the phone when throwing a smaller gathering. It's less expensive than a paper invitation, you usually get a yes or no right away, and it's personal and pleasant.

CLASSIC INVITATION

There are two types of invitations—classic and creative. Go for a classic invitation when throwing a milestone event, like a baptism, wedding, or a fiftieth anniversary. It can also be suitable for a glamorous themed party, like your own Oscar party or Nobel Prize Banquette.

A classic invitation says the party is grand, and the language on the card should be short and direct. Don't write out punctuation marks. Instead start new sentences on a new line. It's a good idea to state the event's attire, even if there is none, just to avoid misunderstandings and stress over what to wear. You can order custom-made classic invitations online, or in your local paper shop. In the shop you will get help and guidelines to assure you get the quality and design you like. If you are on a budget you can easily make your own beautiful knock-off classic invitations at home. Choose a paper of thicker quality; this will give a luxurious feel to your invite. Before starting with your self-made card design, a tip is to head down to the paper store anyway. There you will get lots of ideas and inspiration for a knock-off when looking through their books and selection.

RULES FOR A CLASSIC INVITATION

Color
White or cream colored paper and matching envelopes.

Size
The card should be 4x6 inches, or 5x7 inches.

Design
Keep it simple, preferably with a border around the text. Border and text should be the same color.

Motif
This is an optional small graphic symbol that matches the occasion.

Monogram
Optional—initials on the invitation.

Ink
Use one of the classic colors: black, dark blue, silver, or gold ink.

Text
Align the text to the left, or center it on the card.

Handwritten
Add a personal touch by writing the guest's name on the invitation or address on the envelope by hand, preferably with a calligraphy pen.

Card Facts 101
Are you on a spending spree and want to custom order beautiful invitations from your local paper store? Here are some useful expressions that might help you discuss the look of your card with the store expert.

Card stock—The thickness/weight of the paper, usually ranging from 65–100 pounds

Engraved—A copper stamp is used to raise or lower the paper to create a symbol or text.

Thermography—A technique using chemicals in the ink to raise the text.

CREATIVE INVITATION

USUALLY THE RULE *of thumb is "The crazier, the better," but remember, stick to your theme. A creative invitation is perfect for a birthday or cocktail party and nowadays it's also common to send out creative invitations to parties that traditionally used to have classic invitations. To weddings and baptisms, for example, it's popular to decorate the invitations with dried flowers or bows for a more romantic or cuter look. Let your creativity and style decide what your invitation should look like. Don't* hesitate to experiment with different card folds, choice of colors and papers. Instead of mailing invitation cards, you can also send out things that match your theme. Write your invitations on stickers and attach them to a CD with the matching party-music mix, a lollipop for your sweet night, or whatever you want your invite to be. Make the text fun and upbeat. It can even be a bit outrageous. Try to make lightweight invitations to keep your postage costs down.

Ideas for Creative Invitations

- Photos. Take snapshots of gadgets or yourself dressed up to match the party theme. Go to your local drugstore and have them printed in black and white, or in a brown tint, if you want to create an old-fashioned or different look. Glue or use photo corners to attach them to your cards and make them your invitations.

- Things. Send a compass for a camping party, an oven mitt with the where and when to a barbeque gathering, flip-flops for a beach party, bingo trays welcoming a bingo evening, or a pacifier for the "It's A Boy" party.

- Telegram. A fun, fab, and different way to invite your guests.

- Live Invitations. This is over the top, but if you have a friend volunteering, or the budget for it, don't hesitate to send out live invitations. Have a flower messenger deliver invitations to the midsummer night's party in his bouquets, an opera singer belting out the info for your operetta evening on the guests' doorsteps, or a belly dancer inviting your friends to an exotic brunch while shaking her hips.

INVITATION ETIQUETTE/KNOW-HOW

Whether you choose a classic or creative one, there are some basic rules to remember when putting together an invitation.

Date, Time, Place, and Occasion

Always double-check that your invitation contains this information before sending it out. Convey the same information verbally if you invite your guests over the phone.

RSVP

Let your guests know how you want to be informed if they will be able to attend or not. This is especially important the larger the event gets. Via phone, RSVP card, or email? Choose only one. Also state the last date to RSVP. If you are an extremely polite host you have enclosed a pre-stamped and addressed reply card with your invitation. This is recommended if you want your guests to RSVP with their food choices. Make small boxes on the card where the guests can mark if they want meat, fish, or a vegetarian dish. Also assign a space where they can write if they are allergic to certain foods. This will make your guest list easier to organize.

The Food

Hint as to what will be served so the guests know what to expect. However, don't get too detailed. "Cocktails and Canapés" is enough information for a cocktail party.

Save The Date

Send out the invitations approximately three weeks before your party. People will forget that they are invited if you send them out earlier. If you send them later, the chances are that they already have other plans. If you're preparing a party of mammoth size that no one should miss, you can send a "Save the Date Card" six to eight weeks prior to the party. Let everyone know you are planning a big event and that they should mark their calendars. Three weeks before the bash, send out the real invitation.

VIP

Write a personal note and send it along with the regular invitation if there is a person you really hope to see at your party. It's a friendly gesture and the chance that he or she will attend increases dramatically.

Lists

Make one "A" and one "B" list with names. Start sending invitations to the guests on the "A" list. When you get a feel for how many can make it, start filling up with names from the "B" list. At a larger event, typically 50 percent answer yes on the first mailing.

Invite Away

There are always guests that have to cancel last minute because of cars breaking down, ill children, or overtime at work. Invite one or two extra faces for every ten guests to compensate for these possible no shows. An exception to this rule is when you are having an intimate seated dinner party where you don't invite extra guests.

Bring On the Boys

It's a fact: guys more often decline invitations than girls. Remember to invite more men than women if your ambition is to throw an equally mixed party.

Choose the Right Date

Get your almanac out when picking a party date so you make sure that it doesn't coincide with a friend's birthday or any major holidays. In general, January and July are two bad bash months. During July, your friends are probably away on vacation. Everyone is party-exhausted in January after Thanksgiving, numerous Christmas parties, and New Year's Eve.

What Does RSVP Mean?

RSVP is short for the French expression, Répondez s'il vous plait. Translation: please answer.

Invitation Series Online

www.evite.com
www.sendomatic.com
www.dynamiteinvites.com

DRESS CODE

ATTIRE INDICATES THE *party's level of elegance and puts the guests at ease, so they don't have to worry about being under- or over-dressed. However, if you suspect that your friends aren't familiar with expressions like "black-tie" and "Informal Attire," it's wise to briefly explain their meaning to avoid stress and confusion. Please keep in mind that most people don't have tuxedos with tails or Academy Award– style gowns in their closets and many will decline your invitation if you have too many requirements. If the dress code isn't mentioned on the invitation, it's up to your guests to pick their own party outfits. A good suggestion for the theme party, or if you just want to have fun, is to write expressions like "summer chic," or "dress to the nines" on the invitatons.*

White Tie
A gala celebration! To be honest it's almost never required today unless you attend diplomatic parties or private balls.
Him: Black tailcoat with a white pique vest worn over a formal white shirt is required, as well as black shoes with a spit shine. White gloves on the dance floor are optional.
Her: A long and formal evening gown fit for a princess. Gloves are perfect with this outfit and can be worn when greeting other guests and when dancing, but not when eating.

Black Tie
Most formal events are black-tie gatherings.
Him: A black tuxedo, white shirt, black bow tie, and a black cummerbund is the classic outfit. The folds of the cummerbund should face upward. Today, unless the event is totally old school, you can opt for a lighter and brighter color on the shirt, tux, and bow tie. You can even skip the bow tie entirely if you want.
Her: A less formal long gown or shorter cocktail length dress. Consider the time of the year and the occasion when you pick your dress. Gloves can be used as well.

Formal Attire
"Formal" actually means different things depending on the time the party takes place.
Him: Before 6:00 PM, formal means that the man should wear a dark suit, with a white shirt and a traditional tie that isn't too colorful or crazy. After 6:00 PM, formal

actually means black-tie. See above for directions.
Her: Before 6:00 PM the lady can wear a business type of suit, a dress that isn't an evening gown, or a two-piece outfit like a skirt and a sweater. After 6:00 PM, formal means black-tie.

Informal Attire
Informal doesn't mean casual. Also, the gentlemen's attire depends on the time for the event.
Him: Before 6:00 PM, the man wears a sport coat or a suit of a preferred color, casual shirt and no tie. After 6:00 PM it's still a sport coat or a suit, but in darker colors, with a dress shirt and tie.
Her: A short dress or dressy pants ensemble. Before 6:00 PM, it's ok to choose a colorful outfit. After 6:00 PM, go with a darker one.

Casual
Generally, this means anything goes. Shorts, sandals, and a T-shirt would be a great outfit for the casual pool party. If you want your guests to be neat, pressed, and clean you should write "dressy casual" on the invitation. This means the guests should wear something comfortable, but still a little nicer than something ordinary. Business casual is a common term for networking and business-related events being held right after work. Opt for a crisp and neat look, something you would wear to an important meeting with your CEO.

GIFTS AND GOODIE BAGS

IT'S A TRADITION THAT *the host or hostess gives a small present, like a goodie-bag, when the guests leave the party. It serves as a nice thank-you for coming and as a memory of the event. The gifts can also be placed on the guests' plates as treat, when they sit down for dinner. This way they serve as perfect icebreakers and topics of discussions for the guests around the table.*

Here are some ideas of inexpensive, or totally free, gifts for your guests.

Home baked

Bake something they can indulge in the morning after. Wow them by making your own jam or marmalade that you send along with homemade breads.

Candy

Candy is always a great choice in a gift bag. Even better, try making your own sweets. It feels like a special gesture when wrapped in a cute cone or gift-wrapped box. Another idea is to buy lollipops and decorate them with self-made stickers using pictures, texts, or maybe vintage-inspired bookmarks.

Spa

Visit your favorite spa, tell them about your party, and see if they are willing to provide your party-goers with 15 percent discount cards to their treatments. Inviting the owner usually helps.

Yoga

Do you know someone who knows someone who knows a yoga instructor that wishes to take on more students? Ask the instructor to teach a free class for you and your guests a couple of days after your party. It's great recruiting for the yoga teacher, and great cleansing for you.

Flowers

Create small individual flower arrangements and use them as place cards at the dinner table. Let your guests take them home at the end of the night. For your foodie friends give them planted herbs, or for your gardener pals give them a tulip bulb with a card explaining its origin.

P.S. These gift ideas also work as excellent presents to the host or hostess (instead of that bottle of wine) next time you are invited to a party yourself. If you insist on buying wine, a good rule of thumb is to buy one for about the same price as your age.

DECOR

*D*elicious food, fun guests, and good music would make a great party almost anywhere, but not in New York City. The competition is so cutthroat in the Big Apple that there always has to be something extraordinary about the event to attract guests. Usually "extraordinary" is accomplished by spending lots of time and dollars on fantastic décor.

I've built a belvedere and a fake castle in Central Park for a "Sex and the City" party, draped a penthouse completely in white for Jennifer Lopez's party, rolled out a 250-foot-long lawn on Fifth Avenue when throwing a bash for a handbag company; and once I decorated a photo studio with twenty blooming cherry trees for an event that was photographed by Vogue magazine. Decoration budgets in the hundreds of thousands are nothing unusual for a major event in New York City.

Even at events like these, you'll always end up in some kind of decoration crisis. Mishaps like party tents collapsing when helicopters land too close, or curtains falling down just before the VIP guest Nicolas Cage is supposed to arrive to his very own movie premiere, or a red carpet rolling up, threatening to knock over high-heeled guests such as Reese Witherspoon, Kim Cattrall, or Drew Barrymore. Conclusion: always have handy your first-aid party kit and your toolbox, consisting of must-haves such as a glue and a staple gun, Band-Aids, steel wires, double-sided and duct tape, calligraphy pens, pins, thread, and so on.

BEFORE YOU DECORATE

THE BEST AND *most convenient place for a party is usually your own apartment or house. There is a kitchen where you can prep food, no venue fee, you know where you have everything, and more guests than you think will fit. Move out big and bulky furniture to adjacent rooms that are not being used for the fete, or store them short term with friendly neighbors you've invited.*

With a few simple décor tips, you will quickly be able to turn your living room into a vibrating nightclub, a hot Caribbean island, or any other atmosphere you desire. But first you need to get your space ready for the transformation ...

EMPTY SPACES

Shoes, bills, knick-knacks—put everything that doesn't fit your party's theme, clutters up your space, or is fragile, into a closet or roped off room. Make an extra effort to create clean surfaces on tables, chests, windowsills, and bookshelves. This will make the room feel more spacious, and the guests will have plenty of spots where they can put their drinks.

SKIP THE CLEANING

Use Windex spray to quickly buff up shiny surfaces such as door handles, faucets, tables, and shelves. Don't worry about the dust bunnies under your sofa–no one will notice them anyway. Vacuum and clean properly after the party—there's no need to do it twice.

THE BATHROOM

This is the only room you have to clean thoroughly since almost every guest will pay a visit here. Scrub tiles and shiny areas, stock up on toilet paper and guest towels, and buy a cute, scented candle or draw up a bath and place floating candles in it for atmosphere. A basket with chewing gum, mouthwash, hair spray and other toiletries will be much appreciated by singles during the night. This is always the perfect place for a flower arrangement. Are the bathroom pipes slow? Clean them out before your party.

REFURNISH

Unless you are having a seated reception, arrange furniture (couches, chairs, and armchairs) you want to have in the room into groups. Pillows and blankets are great for building socializing "islands" as well. The seating areas make the party more social and give the space a better "flow" for mingling.

TEMPORARY COAT-CHECK

Tight on closet space? Use a curtain rod and put two chairs together, seats facing each other for balance. Place the rod on top of the chairs, back supports and attach the bar with tape. Put the "coat check" in a separate room.

The bathroom will be one of the party's most popular spots. Give some extra thought by adding a flower arrangement, upscale soaps, luxurious hand lotion, and beautiful candles to boost your party's glam factor.

DECORATING
– 5 essentials

ONCE YOU ARE *finished with the preparations (see p. 36), it's time to decorate your venue. The right party décor puts the guests in the right mood from the very moment they enter.*
Well-crafted and beautiful decorations enhance any event. During daylight events, focus on the details, while at night, concentrate on making bold eye-catching decorations, since defects can be easily hidden in the dark with the correct lighting. The five essentials when decking out your party are: fabric, color, lighting, flowers, and music. Experiment, stick to the theme, and have fun.

1. FABRIC

AN EASY WAY *to change a room and create a new mood is to decorate it with fabrics. You can easily make pillowcases, tablecloths, drapes, cover chair backs, or go with your own creative ideas. Keep these things in mind:*

 PATTERN

Choose a fabric with a pattern that you like, but also matches the party theme. If the event takes place in dark surroundings, go for brighter and stronger colors and bigger patterns than you usually would—otherwise they won't pop.

 THEME COLOR

Pick one of the pattern's colors to serve as the party's thematic color. Use it when deciding on napkins, flowers, trays, what color the cocktails should be, and so on. This makes the party's design feel well planned and thought out.

 ACCENTS

While keeping consistent with your pattern and main thematic color, dare to use totally different materials and palettes in some spots. This makes your design more dynamic and interesting. Fake fur and glitter can spice up a party's design.

 CHEAT

The bigger the party, and the dimmer the ligths, the more you can cheat. Make magic with glue and staple guns, and double-sided tape. Remember, it only has to hold up for one evening! Create new pillowcases by wrapping fabrics around your regular pillows. Use a stapler to make your creations stay in place for the night. A drapery can be easily made by using a thin pole, or an inexpensive curtain rod that can be adjusted into different lengths. Fold the fabric around the pole, staple it together, and hang it up. Tablecloths that match the rest of your décor are quick and easy to make. Cut the fabric in appropriate sizes. Fold in and iron the fringed edges. Glue to make it stay folded.

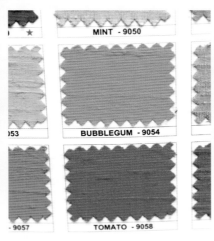

MINT - 9050

053 BUBBLEGUM - 9054

9057 TOMATO - 9058

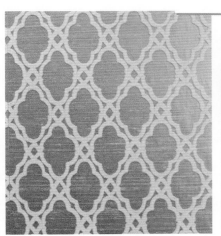

2. CHOICE OF COLOR

COLORS ARE SAID *to affect us subconsciously and evoke different emotional moods. For example, yellow, red, and orange are supposed to stimulate the appetite—something many fast food restaurants have kept in mind. So before you pick your party's prominent color in fabrics, flowers, and lighting, sit down and give your options some thought.*

 WHITE

Symbolizes: Purity, childhood, and virginity.
For the Party: Makes the room bigger and is perfect if you want a neutral mood. Solely white colors give a sterile impression, but combined with bright pastel, silver, crystal, or gold, you easily achieve a classy feel.

 PINK

Symbolizes: Sensitivity, affection, elegance, and sentimentality.
For the Party: Pink is very inviting and sets an atmosphere where your guests want to linger (which is not a good choice if you want them to leave early). Too many bright and pastel pink colors gives a very girly and adolescent touch to the room, which you want to avoid unless you are throwing a teenage bash or a Barbie-themed party.

 ORANGE

Symbolizes: Happiness, optimism, self-confidence and energy.
For the Party: Orange minimizes the room's size and creates a positive, vibrating, and intimate atmosphere.

 RED

Symbolizes: Love, freedom, defiance, and chaos.
For the Party: Red, just like orange, is a vibrating color that brings a lot of energy to a space. A lighter shade of red makes a room more spacious, while a darker nuance makes it smaller and brings a decadent and old-fashioned feel.

 YELLOW

Symbolizes: Delight, happiness, independence, wisdom, and creativity.
For the Party: A color that works year-round and magnifies the size of the venue. If you want a spontaneous and joyful feeling to your party, this is the color to go for.

 GREEN

Symbolizes: Hope, balance, calm, responsibility, and success.
For the Party: When you want a relaxed party with quiet conversation and some jazz tunes playing in the background, go with green. Green is also considered the color for ghosts, monsters, and mermaids—remember that for next Halloween.

 BLUE

Symbolizes: Stability, depth, intellect, and elegance.
For the Party: Said to help people concentrate better and to have a positive effect on the brain overall. Choose blue if you want to encourage your guests to have long and intellectual conversations. Blue also gives a clean and hygienic impression, which is great if you don't have time to make those door knobs shiny before your party. Lighter blue nuances enhance the size of the room.

 BLACK

Symbolizes: Grief, fear, loneliness, and abandonment.
For the Party: Too much black gives a depressing impression, but is perfect when looking to bring out other strong colored objects in your design, make a room smaller, or screen off an area.

3. LIGHTING

THE MOST IMPORTANT *and, at the same time, the most overlooked element of decorating is lighting. You can decorate all day long but if you don't light it properly, your design won't work. Proper illumination will make your décor look amazing, even if you cheat and put it together in a hurry.*

 OVERHEAD LIGHTS

Regular overhead lights are forbidden during parties. Their bright lights are unglamorous and unflattering. Not even colored light bulbs will help. Keep them turned off during the event unless they have dimmer switches.

 SPOTLIGHTS

Get inexpensive spotlights that attach with clips and direct them on your flower arrangements, buffet, or other objects you want to highlight in the room. Use colored bulbs or heat resistant colored film or gels to achieve different moods. Colored bulbs can also be used in your ordinary lamps.

 CANDLES

Nothing creates a cozy and vibrating atmosphere easier than candles. Be generous with wax and wicks, not only on the tables but also in the windows, on trays, the floor, and preferably in clusters to maximize the effect. For safety's sake, assure that nothing flammable is close by and attach the candleholder to its surface with double-sided tape underneath.

 ROPE LIGHTS

Get a kitschy effect by placing rope lights in unusual places, such as under the couch or in a turned off chandelier. Blink the lights and a "disco" feel is guaranteed.

Decoration Tips

- A New Room: Can you attach drawing pins to your ceiling? Congratulations! You can quickly set up a lounge area by using light fabrics hanging from the ceiling to divide up the room. Place pillows on the floor. It's a great effect and will be a popular gathering spot.

- Mirrors: Maximize the effect of your flower arrangements and candles by putting mirrors behind or underneath them. Mirrors in a narrow room create a spacious feel. They also make excellent serving trays and are a fun alternative to regular tablecloths and placemats.

- Scents: Memories and emotions are triggered by scents. Make a spice tray with lit candles and piles of spices for your exotic fete. It smells great and looks fabulous. Throwing a Christmas party? Bake gingerbread cookies just before your guests arrive to get them in a jolly mood.

- DVD: Rent a fireplace on DVD for your after-ski party, Baywatch for the February indoor beach party, and a great Bollywood flick for your Indian affair. It will make your guests smile but also enhances the party's theme.

Outdoor Decorations

Get a glamorous feel by placing pillows, a divan, candles, and other typical indoor objects in your garden. Another tip is to get branches from leafy trees and place them in buckets filled with sand or gravel. If the buckets are old and ugly, cover them with fabrics. With plenty of buckets and branches, you can create interesting outdoor rooms and shielding walls. Protect yourself against unreliable weather by renting a party tent. If the tent looks boring, simply roll up the walls and use fabric to create new walls instead. A budget-friendly alternative is to place four tall sticks in separate sand-filled buckets and stretch a cover over the construction, preferably a waterproof one. This will at least hold off drizzle. During dusk and evening you can create beautiful effects with pitch torches and/or lanterns in the trees.

Smoking

Decide what your rules will be for smoking before the party kicks off. Should the guests go outside, or are they allowed to smoke inside in a restricted area? (For example, next to a window.) Even if you are antismoking, make sure the smoking area is nicely decked out. Have visible ashtrays, preferably tall ones, to mark the spot. Regular flowerpots turned upside down on a plate do the trick as well. Inform your guests when they arrive where they can satisfy their craving for nicotine.

Spruce Up Your Wall

Your white walls can, in a few seconds, be turned into any color to match your party's theme. Simply uplight them using colored spot lights. Or why not buy large cheap artist canvases that you spray-paint with a color or cover with a fabric. Hang them instead of pictures on your walls, both to protect your art and heighten the theme.

Candle Wax

Don't worry about wax spills when decorating with candles. Just freeze it the next day with ice, and then easily remove it.

Design Your Own Candles

Search online or in magazines for images that fit the party's theme. Copy and cut to size, and tape the pictures around regular drinking glasses that you've prepared with tealights inside.

4. FLOWER ARRANGEMENTS

FLOWERS ALWAYS BRING *a wonderful feel to parties, especially at intimate daytime gatherings, where they are easy to spot. Light your floral creations at bigger nighttime parties. Otherwise, they easily "disappear" in the darkness and no one will see your artistic abilities. Is your party a sit-down event, or a standing affair, like a cocktail party? Adjust the placement of your arrangements so they are at your guests' eye level. Arranging flowers is like dressing fashionably. Your blood red skirt is beautiful in the closet, but matched with your neon pink pumps, migraine attacks will follow wherever you go. Don't always choose the flowers you think are the prettiest but look at the whole picture and pick the types that complement each other and suit the party theme. One or two plump flowers that give a lot of color — one type that hangs down if you want to cover the vase, and twigs and grass to create volume and height — are simple, basic steps to follow and many times enough for an arrangement.*

Be careful with mixing too many exotic flowers, since they are difficult to match with each other. Also, show consideration to allergy sufferers by being sparse with strong scented flowers.

HOW TO MAKE YOUR OWN FLOWER ARRANGEMENT

❧ Clean the flower stems when you get home—leaves quickly rot in water and create bacteria. Cut flower stems diagonally so they drink water better. With bushes and twigs, cut a cross in their trunks.

❧ Put the flowers in water a couple of hours before arranging them so they have time to open up. If not, the risk is that the shape of your design will change when they finally do. In a hurry? Use lukewarm water. It will make the flowers open up quicker.

❧ Use wet oasis in the base of the vase instead of water to shape the arrangement easily (and of course less spills are a bonus).

❧ If you are using a water-filled vase, tape a checked pattern on the vase's opening. This will help you spread the flowers evenly as you arrange.

❧ Place the vase at eye level when creating your arrangement. Shape a round and even form to look like half a ball. Rotate the vase to make sure your design is how you want it to look from each and every angle. Don't forget to look at the form underneath to make sure the edge is even.

❧ Not everyone wants their arrangements to have the shape of a half ball. Don't be afraid to experiment with heights and shapes. You can also mix in other materials such as feathers, straws of reed, sparkling spray, and much more.

❧ When you're done, place the flowers in a cool spot. It will help them keep their shape and freshness until the party starts.

GREAT PARTY FLOWERS

PEONIES
Great—and an evening party favorite with its grand and colorful flowers. Just a few are enough to make the arrangement plump and magnificent. Can be found in a variety of different colors.

RANUNKLE
Colorful, but more petite and fragile then peonies. Perfect for a daytime event.

ROSES
The classic of classics, and can be used in many different ways. Put on your gardening gloves and stroke alongside the stems to get rid of the thorns before arranging them.

TULIPS
Are always "in" and can be found in every imaginable color. A great choice for parties that take place during the day.

CARNATIONS
The dreaded prom flower is back in style. Ideal when making creative forms using oasis. Carnations also stay fresh a long time. The drawback is that they are difficult to match with other flowers, and are usually best used on their own.

LILLIES
Dramatic and great for the evening party. Remove the pollen pastilles before you arrange them so the guests don't get painted in yellow when they smell your beautiful flora. Be careful with heavy scented ones like Casablanca. Guests can get dizzy, feel discomfort, and get allergic reactions.

TWIGS AND LEAVES
Gives beautiful height and a creative, festive, and striking look to your arrangments. Buy or pick your own twigs, add a few tulips, and voila! You have a super easy and pretty spring arrangement. Leaves give a splendid display of colors to your fall arrangement.

Flower Hearts and Disco Balls
Want to make an arrangement out of the ordinary? Cut dry oasis into the outline you want. Wrap the oasis in chicken wire before wetting it and sticking flowers into it. The wire makes sure that the ceiling hanging arrangement keeps its shape and doesn't fall apart onto the heads of admiring guests.

Oasis
Oasis is a condensed foam that you stick flowers in. Buy oasis at your local florist. With it you easily achieve desired shapes and heights for your arrangements. Soak the oasis for at least 30 minutes before you put in the flowers. No additional water is needed.

Budget Tips
To save on vases you can use regular water glasses. Use them as they are with their different shapes, sizes, and colors. Cover their insides with leaves, or their outside with colored paper, to achieve your desired effect. You don't always have to use expensive cut flowers from the florist when decorating your party. Potted plants in regular terracotta pots are a less expensive alternative that look great. Spruce up the pots with ribbons, fabrics, or tissue paper. Hyacinths and azaleas are popular potted plants and pretty to use as decorations.

The Restroom
You should always put flowers here. It makes the bathroom more attractive, more fragrant, and is the bouquet your guests will look at the longest.

At the Dinner Table
Tall arrangements are great, but not on the dining table. Make low compositions so the guests can see each other and not just leaves and flowers when eating. A single flower handpicked in your garden, or a few arranged in a mini bouquet at each plate, gives a warm and welcoming impression. The alternative is to make extremely high arrangements on top of very narrow stems.

Quantity, Please
Just like candles, several bouquets grouped together make a striking impression. Vary size and height, but remember to keep a consistent theme with the flowers.

Tape
Attach vases placed on risky spots with double-sided tape to the surface they're on. This will prevent them from falling if they are bumped into.

Blooming Chandelier
Overhead lights should always be turned off during an event. If you have a chandelier, use it to hang flowers instead.

Variation
Don't fixate on making all arrangements look the same. Variation makes the room interesting. Just have a theme they all follow, like a color scheme or a specific flower that is found in each arrangement. Using the same flower, but in a variety of different vases clustered together, is simple but striking.

Clear Vases
These vases are inexpensive and can be found in a variety of shapes and sizes. A downside is that the stems and oasis show through and can be difficult to cover if the vase is tall.

Tip! Big leaves on the inside of the vase give a great effect while hiding ugly stalks. By using leaves in new shapes or colors your vase gets a different look.

Call the Florist
Tulips are more expensive in the winter than during the spring. Pick up the phone and ask which flowers are in season to find the best prices. Don't forget to warn your florist if you want lots of a certain flower so he/she can be sure to have them in stock.

5. PARTY MUSIC

Great music does wonders for a party. It fills the room with energy and reinforces the party's theme. Music also helps the guests to relax and feel at ease. The basic rule is to always play music, even at a sit down dinner, but go easy on the volume. Your guests should be able to talk to each other in a normal tone of voice. In order to avoid rushing to the stereo and changing tracks every three minutes, try burning your own CDs. If your computer has powerful speakers and iTunes or similar music software, you can easily compose a suitable playlist for your party. Pick tunes you enjoy

yourself, but also be considerate to your guests. If you are a huge fan of heavy metal, feel free to include a few of your favorite tracks, but mix it up with songs appealing to a wider audience. If you're shaking your stuff all by yourself on the dance floor, it's probably a good indication that you should consider playing something else.

If you can't burn your own CD or play music files on a computer, head to your local record store and check out the movie soundtrack section. Sound-tracks are specially written to evoke a certain mood and usually stick to that theme for over an hour. Choose a record that suits your party. If your budget allows, nothing can beat a live band at a party. Even the most boring Christmas party will rock if some reckless amateurs go on stage and interpret classic holiday songs.

Old classic hits are safe bets if you want to see some sweat on the dance floor.

THE VENUE

SOMETIME IT'S NECESSARY *to throw the party outside your home's four walls, either for practical reasons or because you just really want to try a new environment. Parties at venues can be extremely expensive if you go for an old mansion or a French castle, but there are also plenty of inexpensive and fabulous alternatives.*

The Art Gallery
These funky premises always have great lightning, and it's a win-win situation. You get a fun venue for your party while the gallery owner exposes his art to prospective costumers. Ask if you can borrow the gallery for free or for a discounted price. Perfect for a larger cocktail party with twenty-five guests or more.

The Spa or Shop
Is it possible for your favorite spa or shop to stay open a few extra hours for a night? While you're there, maybe they can even give you and your guests a 10 to 20 percent discount. The company gets great PR, the guests get a bargain, and you get a new venue for your event. Perfect for a girls' night out.

The Miniature Golf Course
Book the whole course for you and your friends. Make it an early-bird event, and you'll get a good deal. Bring your old boom box from the 80s. Play music, golf among windmills and waterfalls, mingle, and sip on drinks. Perfect PG event that all ages will enjoy.

The Night Club
Bars and night clubs want guests and are therefore willing to rent their spaces for a good price, or even for free since they will make a good profit on the food and alcohol they sell. Have the party in the middle of the week, and it is easier to find a bargain. Always negotiate on everything, even the alcohol. If you don't rent out the whole place, make sure you get your own VIP room or section. It's more exciting if you decide on a place that recently opened. Be sure to scout the location first though. Perfect venue if you have a lot of guests but not a lot of bucks.

In the Open
If you trust in the weather gods, your possibilities are endless. You can host amazing parties on the beach, by the pool, in the park, garden, ski slope, and so on.

TABLE SETTING

One of the most important table settings I designed was for an event hosted by the Food Network and Home and Garden TV. It took place on the ninety-eighth-floor penthouse in one of Donald Trump's skyscrapers. The enormous apartment was raw, and we decorated it from scratch to actually make it look like a glamorous home for one evening. We ended up renting antique furniture, parts of TV sets, and even books by the yard. Imagine getting all that up to the ninety-eighth-floor! I collaborated with TV hosts from Home and Garden TV on the interior, and with Rachel Ray, Emeril, Bobby Flay, and the other Food Network stars on what was served. One of the HGTV hosts had seen gorgeous green granite plates that she just had to have for the party. My task was to find 150 of them, and after a long search I finally found them in California. Not only did they cost a small fortune, but we also had to ship them express via truck across the country to NYC. But in the end, it was worth it. They looked fantastic on the dinner table!

At another party the socialite hostess refused to have regular salt and pepper shakers on the tables. She insisted they had to be silver, from Cartier. When she first told me, I thought it sounded crazy, but now the shakers are my favorites as well.

For a luxury jewelry-brand dinner, I had almost a thousand white roses sprayed with the company's logo in gold. The arrangement was a success, and I was asked to do a feature story in Brides magazine about how to monogram everything from spoons to leaves with Swarovski crystals.

HOW TO SET YOUR TABLE

DON'T PANIC IF *your dinner set doesn't have enough pieces to accommodate all your guests. Even if you don't have enough plates, it's trendy to mix and match vintage china and table pieces to get a striking effect. It's also a much more appealing alternative than paper and plastic. To ensure your set-up doesn't look cluttered, use single-colored base pieces in, for example, white.*

If you don't want to risk smashing your grandmother's antique soup tureen during your dinner party, you can always rent china from rental companies. It will add to your budget, but the nice part is that you don't have to do the dishes afterwards. It's a fact: at parties, things break and get dirty. Therefore, always have back-up plates, tablecloths, cutlery, and other props. Always have extra glasses: 25 percent extra for a dinner party, and at least 100 percent extra for a cocktail party.

THE DINNER PLATE

Place the plate approximately one inch from the table's edge. This rule can be tricky to follow if you have a round table.

THE CHARGER

If you are hosting a fancy dinner, you should place a large decorative charger plate on the table as a base. On top of the charger, place the plates for the starter and main course. Remove it before serving dessert.

THE BREAD PLATE

This is a small plate, placed to the side and used for serving bread. The butter knife should be laid horizontally across the plate, and remember to place butter on the table before the guests arrive. If the table is small, this is the first plate to go.

NAPKINS

You can place the napkins wherever you like. On top of the dinner plates, next to the cutlery, or even on the chair backs. Be creative.

GLASSES

During dinner it's common to use several different glasses: one glass for white wine, another for red, and one for water. Place your glasses above the dinner plate slightly to the right since most guests are right handed. The glasses should be placed in the order they are to be used, with the first glass to be used to the left of the water glass that is always positioned far right.

FORKS

If you want to set your table Americana style, place the forks to the left of the plate with the prongs facing upwards. Turn the forks around, so the prongs face into the table, and voila! You've made a French setting. When using numerous forks, place the one that the guest should start with to the far left. A starter fork should be smaller than the main course's. A proper hostess never places more than three forks next to her plates, not counting the dessert fork placed above the plate. If she needs more forks, she brings them to the table when they are to be used. However, at a very grand affair with lots of guests, it's best to have all the forks on the table from the start to make the dinner run smoothly, even if there are more than three.

KNIVES

Place your knifes to the right of your plate. When using more than one knife, put the first one to be used to the far right. The knives' edges should always face the plate.

Sometimes it's fun to think outside the box when you set your table. For example, use a picture frame instead of regular tablecloth (se

This rule also goes for any possible butter spreaders. The starter knife should be smaller than the ones used for the main course. Correct etiquette is to never set the table with more than two knives next to the plate, not counting the butter spreader. If more than two knives are needed, bring them in just before they are to be used. At big events, it is okay to cheat and have more than two knives on the table from the start to make serving easier.

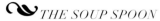 THE SOUP SPOON

Place the spoon to the far right, outside the knives.

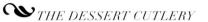 THE DESSERT CUTLERY

Proper etiquette is to set the table with both a dessert spoon and fork. The utensils are placed on the table before the meal, just above the plate. If you are having a shortage of cutlery choose the one you have the most of.

THE COFFEE SET

At larger dinners, save time by placing the coffee cup on the table before the meal. Set it behind the water glass so it's not in the way during the meal. Lay the spoon on the plate to the right. Milk and sugar are put on the table when the dessert or cake is being served. A nice alternative is to bring out the cups just before the dessert, but prepare trays in advance with cups, milk, and sugar to make the transition as easy as possible.

Asian Table Setting

Use bowls instead of plates, and chopsticks instead of cutlery. If you place the chopsticks directly on the table you have a Chinese setting. By placing the tip of the sticks onto a little stone, or ceramic cube, you have a Japanese setting. Place everything on a low table so you can sit on pillows instead of chairs.

When Accidents Happen

At the website www.replacementsltd.com you can find parts for your set if anything breaks. The site has a large selection. Some plates, glasses, and cutlery are more than 100 years old!

Table Manners

There isn't really an elegant way to correct someone's manners. The best way is to set a good example yourself. Here are some tips:

– Don't bring anything extra to the table, like a half full cocktail glass, cigarettes, or unfinished canapés. Hang your handbag on the back of your chair, or place it on the floor under your stool.

– Put the napkin in your lap and leave it there throughout the dinner. Don't blow your nose in it! If you have to leave the table, put the napkin on the seat.

– When you're finished eating, place the knife and fork together as if the plate was a clock, and the utensils are the hands showing twenty minutes past four. If you just need to take a short break, you place them twenty minutes before four. Never put used utensils on the tablecloth. When finished eating feel free to put the napkin on the table.

– Don't salt and pepper your food before tasting it.

– Eat European style by placing the food on the rounded backside of the fork. It's considered quite posh. Eating American style, using the ladled front of the fork, is many times easier.

– Don't cut all your meat or fish at once. Two pieces at the same time is more than enough.

– Feel free to lean your forearms on the table's edge. But please, no elbows on the table.

– Never pick your teeth at the table. Not even when trying to hide your action with your hand or a napkin.

– Stay calm even if someone spills on your best tablecloth. First, ensure the guest that it doesn't matter (even if it does) and then clean up as much possible. Don't use fabrics and dining sets that can't handle a spill or a crack. Almost every party has a few accidents.

– Take one sip at a time from your drink or wine.

– When drinking white wine, hold the glass at the stem to keep it chilled longer. While indulging in red wine, served room temperature, hold the bowl.

1

2

3

4

5

6

NAPKINS

A NICELY FOLDED *napkin is an easy way to enhance the general look of your table setting. Fabric napkins are preferable. If you don't have any of your own you can easily sew some up. Since you don't need much yardage, treat yourself to a fabric of high quality such as silk or linen. Standard napkin sizes are twelve, fourteen, and sixteen inches. Play around with different fabrics and get two napkins in one with different fabrics on each side. In the long run it's cheaper to use cloth napkins than disposable paper napkins.*

Napkins can be more than just pretty—use them to hold a menu, small gift, or beautiful flower.

IDEAS FOR NAPKIN FOLDS
(see opposite page)

1. A practical and simple fold for the buffet. Attach a ribbon around the napkin and put the cutlery underneath it.

2. An easy fold turns extraordinary when you experiment with different materials. This napkin has a leaf instead of a fabric strap and a brooch to hold it in place.

3. For the fancy dinner you can place the menu in the napkins. This will give your guests something to talk about.

4. Buy wax from a stationery store and use it to spruce up old napkins or thicker paper napkins since it stains.

5. Look through drawers and cupboards and decorate with your finds. Tufts, dried flowers, bookmarks, rhinestones . . .

6. Turn your napkin into a seating card.

Linen Facts

If you have old beautiful linen napkins and tablecloths, use them! It won't hurt them, and it's better then just letting them lay in the cupboard waiting for moths. Here is some general advice on how to keep your linens fresh:

– Never put anything but completely clean and stain-free napkins back into the cupboard or drawer. Even washed stains will attract moths.

– New linen is washed in 140°F water for as short a time as possible. Never tumble dry. Go for a perborate and brightener-free detergent.

– To brighten and clean old linens, put them in room temperature water overnight, then wash by hand. Roll the linen in towels to remove excessive water and let dry.

– Linen is best when it's allowed to dry outside, but avoid drying in direct sunlight.

– Roll up the napkins or press them flat. Don't hot iron them over their folds since this will make them fragile.

– Keep them in a dark cupboard with a few bags of lavender for freshness.

TABLECLOTHS

FEEL FREE TO *skip the tablecloths when having a party. If you have a beautiful tabletop, show it off and use placemats as colorful cliques. Picture frames and mirrors can also work wonders as alternatives to table-cloths.*

However, many do prefer setting a table with fabric. Warm colored and patterned tablecloths add a welcoming feel, while the classic white cloth gives a stark look. Reflect over what your table should look like to fit your theme.

A good thing about tablecloths is that they protect your tabletops from stains or cover already existing ones. They are also good for minimizing sharp sounds from glasses and silverware.

There isn't a rule for how long a tablecloth should be, so simply trust your personal taste when picking out your cover. Keep in mind that the fabric needs at least ten inches on all four sides to get a beautiful drop, and a thirty inch drop is pretty standard. To find your size, measure the table's length and width. If you want ten inches of drop you add on twenty inches to the length and width before picking out your tablecloth. If you are using a round table you simply measure the diameter.

Placemats

Want to set your table with placemats but don't have any? Use what you can find. Colorful and fun patterned cloth napkins are perfect. Picture frames with beautiful motifs, cutting boards, graphic trays, and banana leaves also make great placemats. Be creative.

Design Your Tablecloth

Got a great tablecloth or a piece of fabric you love, but it's not big enough to cover the whole table? Use it anyway. Set the table with a discreetly colored fabric as your base, and then add the decorative cloth.

Box the Table

Long tablecloths that go all the way down to the floor will have extra fabric wrinkled up in the corners. Box the table if you want a more austere silhouette.
1. Take the overflowing fabric hanging in the corner and stretch it out into a wing, so the creases even out.
2. Pull the wing diagonally to the rear.
3. Place your hand on the middle of the wing and fold it in under the tablecloth that is lying flat on the table.
4. Even out and make adjustments with pins if necessary.

Tip! By boxing a regular white sheet you quickly get a classic-looking tablecloth, and no one will know the difference.

Guests & Tablecloth Chart

How many guests can I fit around a 60-inch round table? This chart will tell you, plus provide you with tablecloth sizes for a 30-inch drop.

Round Tables:	Seats	Max	Tablecloth
30″	2	4	90″ diameter
36″	4	5	96″
48″	6	8	108″
54″	7	9	114″
60″	8	10	120″
66″	9	11	126″
72″	10	12	132 ″

Square Tables:	Seats	Max	Tablecloth:
36″ x 36″	4	6	96″ x 96″
48″ x 48″	6	8	108″ x108″
60″ x 60″	8	10	120″ x 120″
72″ x 72″	10	12	132″ x 132″

Rect. Tables:	Seats	Max	Tablecloth:
6′ x 36″	8	8	132″ x 96″
6′ x 42″	8	10	132″ x 102″
8′ x 36″	10	10	156″ x 96″
8′ x 42″	10	12	156″ x 102″

TABLE SEATING

WHEN YOU HAVE *ten guests or more gathered for dinner it's nice to assign seats. It makes the table more dynamic, and with a little thought from you, guests end up next to dining partners they share common interests with. Most hosts and hostesses break into hot flashes as soon as they hear the word seating chart. Relax, it's not a life or death matter, nor is it rocket science. There are actually only three simple rules to keep in mind when you seat guests for a regular dinner party.*

1. Guests should be seated alternating men and women.
2. Each gentleman's lady is seated to his left.
3. Couples are never each other's partners, unless it's their wedding.

The rest is common sense. Try not to seat a hunter next to a passionate vegan, unless you believe that heated discussions are the way to create a memorable dinner pary.

Always wait until the day before the party to compose your seating so possible last-minute changes on the guest list are included.

To make planning easier, draw a table chart on a paper and number the tables. If possible it's great to laminate the sheet. Write down your guest's name on stickers. One color for the ladies, another for the gents. The laminated surface makes it easier to move around the stickers if you change your mind during the process or want to try different solutions. If you have a large group of guests it's a good idea to set up a separate table at your party where you place the name cards from A–Z. Pin a silk ribbon over the cards so they stay put. On each name card, designate the guest's table number, so he or she easily can find their table. Frame the table numbers, and place the frames on each table. Then, place cards at each seat, indicating where the guest is sitting. Round tables are beautiful, but keep in mind that they take up more space and don't seat as many guests as rectangular or square tables. Remember to make every guest feel included at the party. If you invite someone last minute, due to cancellations, make sure that person gets a good seat where he or she feels warmly welcomed. If you still dread seating charts, here are some shortcuts:

❧ *SEATING SHORTCUT 1*

Number the Tables

If you have more then two tables, number them and divide the guests into equal amounts of groups. Put individuals you believe will have a nice time together in the same groups but try to avoid good friends and couples at the same table. They will likely spend most of their time talking to each other. Spread the storytellers evenly around the room. Arrange a name card table assigning table numbers, but at the table let the guests seat themselves. To seat your guests male, female, male, you can use colored napkins, cards that say "Reserved for a Lady," or gifts at each plate that differ for men and women.

❧ *SEATING SHORTCUT 2*

Random

If you don't have the time or energy to think about seating, you can always let chance decide. Try using a deck of cards. If you've invited twenty people, draw ten cards and divide each card into two halves. Ladies and gents that draw the same card get each other at the table. When the number of guests is uneven, you become the joker with a predetermined seat.

Seats

Just a few chairs are enough at a cocktail party since the idea is that guests should stroll around and mingle. At a bigger buffet party, approximately 50 percent of the guests should be able to sit down. For a brunch, smaller buffet, tea party, or dinner gathering, you need seats for each and every guest.

The Twenty-Inch Rule

Each guest should have at least twenty inches of "private" table space from left to right when sitting down. Are you having parallel tables where the guest has a neighbor behind her? The free space between the backs of the chairs when both guests are seated should be twenty inches as well. The distance is necessary if anyone needs to leave the table.

Place Markers

Instead of traditional place cards, experiment with unique place markers. Write on driftwood, shells, jam jars, cards attached to roses, glasses that the guests can take home with them, or on cookies using frosting. However, if the party has a classic-style invitation, the place markers should match the paper and design from the invitation.

Weddings

A wedding's seating differs from a regular party (many times a head table is being used).

– The bride and the groom are always seated in the middle of the wedding's head table. The bride sits to her groom's left.
– The bride has her father to her left. To his left is the mother of the bride.
– The groom has his mother to his right. To her right is the groom's father.
– On the bride's end of the head table is the best man. On the groom's side the maid of honor.
– Guests closely related to the bride and groom should be seated near the top table.
– If parents have been divorced and remarried, it's a good idea to invite some family of the step-parent(s) and put the extra moms and dads at that table close to the top table with some of their relatives.
– Many find these head table arrangements very sensitive and tricky. A good alternative is the so-called "Sweetheart Table," where only the bride and groom are seated. This way you avoid all possible top table drama.

BAR

The "You're Hired!" is the most expensive cocktail I've ever tasted. Mixed with cognac from Napoleon's days, black raspberry liqueur, and grape vodka, the pricy drink costs one thousand dollars when ordered in Donald Trump's The World Bar. I tried one when I was attending a party celebrating the mogul's TV show, The Apprentice. There was, of course, also a "You're Fired!" which cost less than ten bucks.

If the "You're Hired!" is my best cocktail memory, my worst is from a party I put together for a high-end photography magazine. I was so proud of my new martini recipe, made from pomegranate and black grape juice, but I hadn't actually tried the drink myself. While it was being passed around I noticed that guests started to stick their tongues out at each other, and that both their teeth and tongues had turned black. Oops! There was nothing else to do but play dumb and hide in the kitchen. Needless to say the celebrities didn't smile much for the photographers that evening, but the drink sure was yummy.

COCKTAILS

ALWAYS MAKE SURE *your guests are greeted with a drink when they enter the party. The drink puts them at ease, gives them something to do with their hands, and makes everyone less nervous. A drink also works as a great ice-breaker between two people "Oh! You picked the red one, what flavor is that?" Using a cocktail shaker and mixing each drink separately looks fab, but if you don't have a professional bartender on hand it can take forever and get rather messy. Instead, premixed cocktails in pitchers allow you to quickly pour multiple cocktails without spills. Premixing cocktails also allows you to control the alcohol content, which is great for your budget. Always, always, always, have a nonalcoholic alternative on hand as well.*

THE DO-IT-YOURSELF BAR

If balancing fancy trays around all night isn't for you, then the self-help bar is a great and social alternative. Let your guests do the work for you and look stylish as they shake it behind the bar, mixing up their favorite cocktails all night long. This is your guide to building your own DIY bar:

 TABLE

Choose a table that's long and narrow. 6 or 8 ft by 30 or 36 inches wide is usually good.

 LOCATION

Place the table in a spot where there is room for people to gather and has easy access since there will be a lot of refilling traffic going on here.

 ALCOHOL

Place the alcohol bottles on trays, and put the trays in the middle of the table. This way the bottles can be reached from many different angles at the same time.

 MIXERS & ICE

Double up on everything, and place the juice, soda, syrup, other mixers, and ice on each side of the alcohol. These will be your two mixing stations. Also, place your cocktail shakers and bar tools here.

GARNISHES

Cherries, pickled onions, lime and lemon wedges, straws, and other garnishes the guests can add to their drinks are placed in decorative containers next to the mixers and ice.

 GLASSES & NAPKINS

Put the glasses on trays and cocktail napkins on plates at the table's edge where they can be easily reached.

COCKTAIL RECIPES

Find or create recipes that use alcohol and mixers you are serving on your do-it-yourself bar. Write down or print the recipes and place them framed on the table so the guests can be their own bartenders. You can also leave out a bartending guide.

A COMPLETE BAR

"The Big 7" is what makes a bar complete. This means a full bar should contain the following alcohols: vodka, gin, rum, tequila, whiskey, brandy, and liqueur. Building a full bar from scratch is expensive, and when it is finally complete, do you really want to serve your rare cognac at the party? A great and less expensive alternative is to make a bar out of one type of spirit (for example, flavored vodka). Before the party, put berries, spices, fruit or whatever is in season in vodka and let it soak for a couple of days. Before using the vodka, simply strain off the flavoring and serve in shot glasses on a bed of ice. Rum, gin, and tequila are other popular "one spirit" bars.

"THE BIG 7"

Vodka – Most vodkas are produced from grain, but can also be made from potatoes. Usually the alcohol is strained through charcoal to extract impurities and produce a beverage as tasteless as possible. Vodka from Eastern Europe has an oily texture and sweet taste, while Finnish vodka is considered to be the most pure.

Gin – A distinctly flavored dry spirit that derives its character from juniper berries, as well as hints of coriander and citrus. The spirit is believed to have been invented in Holland sometime during the 17th century where it was sold in chemist stores for good health. During the Thirty Years' War, British soldiers brought the spirit back home and called it "Dutch courage." Dry gin is most common today, but there is also a sweet version, called Old Tom, used when mixing the cocktail Tom Collins.

Liqueur – A sweet flavored spirit originally composed to camouflage poor tasting alcohol. During the 14th century people even believed that liqueur, made from vodka flavored with honey and herbs, protected against the Plague. (Of course, the mixture didn't work— 26 million Europeans died.) Liqueurs come in all different strengths, and there is an endless list of flavors that can be used: coffee, almond, orange, peach, vanilla, chocolate, cherry, liquorish, and so on.

Rum – The world's most common spirit. Rum originates from the West Indies but is produced today wherever sugar cane grows. There are two main rum varieties: Rhum Agricole, which is made exclusively out of sugar cane juice, and Rhum Industrial, referring to rums made out of molasses. The molasses rums generally have a neutral taste and are in most cases translucent. Many rums use spices to achieve characteristic flavors.

Tequila – Hundreds of years ago, the Aztec Indians of Latin America enjoyed a fermented beverage made out of the sap from the agave plants. They called this beverage pulque. When the Spanish arrived they brought with them the art of distillation, and after running out of their brandy supply, they started experimenting with the locals' blue agave plant. Their quest to produce a spirit out of the plant succeeded in the town of Tequila, and to this day Tequila can only be produced in this area. Silver and gold tequilas are not aged. Reposado is aged a minimum of two months, but less than a year in oak barrels, and añejo is aged between one and three years. It's a common misunderstanding that Tequila is made out of a cactus when the agave plant actually is an amaryllis. Mezcal resembles Tequila but has more of a smoky taste and is produced all over Mexico with many different types of agave. Mescal usually contains a signature "worm" or larvae at the bottom . . . so please, sip slowly.

Whiskey – Produced world wide with different regional characteristics, Irish whiskey is primarily made from barley and wheat. The mash is dried over coal to get a smooth flavor, while its Scottish cousin is dried over peat which gives it a distinct smoky flavor. What the two countries have in common is that they both age the whiskey in oak barrels for at least three years. Bourbon is the most famous American whiskey, and its main ingredient is corn. Bourbon is aged on burnt oak barrels for two years minimum. Its aging process gives it a burned flavor with a hint of vanilla.

Brandy – Distilled wine that has been aged in oak barrels. Cognac, the most famous brandy, is produced in a French region with the same name that has chalk rich soil. To know how long a cognac has been aged you have to decode the label. VS or *** means 2 years; VSOP or VO, 5 years; and XO or Napoléon, 6 years. These are minimum aging requirements. Most of the time the cognac has been aged even longer.

BAR MUSTS

 Ice

An important ingredient that adds more to your drink then you think. Estimate aproximately one pound of ice per person to have enough for both drinks and possible ice baths. Icebaths are the best way to cool beverages like beer and wine if you are having a bigger party. Dig out a tub, fill it half way with ice, and about 1/8 of the way with water. Add the bottles, and leave them to cool in the bath for approximately thirty minutes or until they have reached desired temperature. Another alternative is to put the bottles in your washing machine and pour ice over them. This way, the melting water will go straight down the drain, and at the end of the evening you won't have to lift and empty heavy tubs. If you want to show off a little bit you can make your own specialty ice cubes for your bar that match your party's theme. Make cubes out of orange juice, or put jelly beans or small flowers in the ice-cube tray before adding water. Ice actually adds flavor to a drink. (For example, a martini that has been shaken with ice has a totally different flavor from one that hasn't been flavored with it.) Usually ice cubes are preferred in cocktails since they melt slowly. Crushed ice is used only for frozen drinks.

Fruit

Works both as a decoration and flavor enhancer. High quality alcohol brands can be expensive. So for your next mixed drink party, get the cheap stuff and simply use high-end freshly squeezed juices and homemade fruit purées. You will save some dough without skimping on any of the flavor. Don't be afraid to experiment using exotic fruits for your drinks.

Tools

Indispensable must-have bar tools are the following: a tall cocktail spoon to stir drinks with, a shaker, cocktail strainer, a small paring knife for your fruits, a small cutting board, tongs for fruit and ice, a wine opener, and finally, a bottle opener (preferably with a spiked tip for opening juice cans as well).

CLASSIC COCKTAILS

THERE ARE ALWAYS *new seasons and trends in cocktails. However, these recipes have been around for decades and are always popular at a party. Guests love them because they've heard of them but often never tried them.*

1 SIDE CAR

1 oz brandy or congac
1 oz Cointreau
1 oz fresh lemon juice

My personal favorite to serve at a classic cocktail party.

1. Burn an orange peel over a cocktail glass to extract a strong citrus flavor. (See p. 73) Save the peel to use for garnish.
2. Shake all the ingredients over ice in a cocktail shaker, and strain the mixture into the cocktail glass.
3. Garnish with the orange peel.

2 MODERN TOM COLLINS

1½ oz gin
1 oz fresh lemon juice
1 oz simple syrup
Club soda
Cherry, and an orange
  slice for garnish

The original drink was so popular at the turn of the century that a special Collins glass was made for it. Sweet gin was used for a time, but now regular gin is commonly used.

1. Shake the gin, lemon juice, and simple syrup over ice in a cocktail shaker. Strain over a highball glass filled with ice.
2. Top off with club soda.
3. Garnish with the cherry and orange slice.

Simple Syrup

Mix equal parts water and sugar in a sauce-pan. Stir over medium heat until the sugar dissolves. Perfect to sweeten drinks with and guaranteed lump free.

3 COSMOPOLITAN

1½ oz citron vodka
¾ oz Cointreau or Triple
  sec
1 oz cranberry juice
½ oz fresh lime juice
Burnt orange peel

A modern classic that became popular when Absolut Citron was launched, and became world famous with help from the TV series Sex and the City. Can be served "up" (without ice) as well as "on the rocks" (with ice).

1. Burn an orange peel over a cocktail glass.
2. If you want to serve the cocktail up, shake all the ingredients in a cocktail shaker and strain into a cocktail glass.
3. If you want to serve the cocktail on the rocks, add all the ingredients in a highball glass filled with ice and stir with a cocktail spoon.
4. If you find the drink too strong, add simple syrup to the mix.

4 MANHATTAN

2 oz whiskey
1 oz sweet vermouth
1 dash Angostura bitter
1 cherry

The legend says that the drink was invented at the Manhattan Club by a bartender named Rob Roy when they where throwing a party for Winston Churchill's mother, Jennie. It has a very distinct flavor.

1. Add all the ingredients into a mixing glass with ice.
2. Stir with a spoon and strain over a cocktail glass when chilled.
3. Garnish with a cherry.

5 CHAMPAGNE COCKTAIL

1 tsp Angostura bitter
1 sugar cube
Lemon peel for garnish
Champagne

Bubbles are the universal symbol for parties and are the perfect ingredient in a "before dinner drink" since they help stimulate appetite. You can always substitute sparkling wine for champagne.

1. Pour the Angostura bitter on top of the sugar cube and let it absorb.
2. Add the sugar cube to the bottom of a champagne glass.
3. Slowly pour the champagne over the sugar cube, holding the glass at a slight angle. The sugar cube will make extra bubbles, and gives the cocktail a flavor of cardamom. Garnish with a lemon peel.
4. If you want to show off you can always burn the lemon peel over the glass before you compose the cocktail.

Burnt Citrus Peel

By burning the peel of a lemon, orange, or lime you derive a citrus-oil that is rich in flavor. Here's how you do it: wash the citrus fruit and cut out a dollar coin-sized peel round. Avoid cutting too deep since you want to avoid the bitter white part of the peel. Hold the peel a few inches above with the colored side facing into the glass. Light a match and hold it between the peel and the glass. Squeeze and the oil will spurt out into the cocktail glass. A great crowd pleaser that also enhances the flavor.

6 MARTINI

3 oz of vodka or gin
¼ oz of vermouth (if you want a dry martini then use dry vermouth)
Olive

Possibly the most famous drink of them all and can be mixed using either vodka or gin as a base. No matter what James Bond says, a martini should always be stirred not shaken.

1. Add the ingredients to a mixing glass filled with ice.
2. Stir about fifty times if you are using large ice cubes, and about twenty-five if you are using smaller cubes.
3. Strain the ice and pour into its signature glass. Garnish with an olive or two, preferably without the pimento in the middle.

Bubbly

Want to glam-up your party? Serve small portion-sized bottles of champagne or sparkling wine. Skip the glasses and simply use straws. It looks so fab it doesn't matter if you serve champagne or just sparkling wine. Movie director Sofia Coppola even sells her own wine, Sofia Mini, in a cool pink can.

1 Side Car 2 Tom Collins 3 Cosmopolitan 4 Manhattan 5 Champagne Cocktail 6 Martini

You can easily strengthen the theme of your event by decorating the serving trays.

WHICH GLASS?

Martini Glass—is used for all "up" cocktails, or drinks served without ice cubes in the glass.

Highball Glass—is for all mixed drinks that are served with ice cubes in the glass. Also used for soda and beer.

Rocks Glass—is for drinks served "on the rocks," a single spirit poured straight over ice cubes with no mixers.

Wine Glass—is used for red and white wine and for frozen cocktails made with crushed ice.

Port Glass—is used to serve port, liqueur, or a high-shelf spirit "straight up" without ice.

Champagne Glass—is for champagne, sparkling wine, and champagne cocktails.

HOW MUCH DO I NEED?

Estimate two drinks per guest during the first hour of the party. For the following hours, estimate one drink per guest per hour.

– One bottle of champagne (750 ml) equals approximately six glasses, but if you are performing a toast, fill the glasses only to one-third of the way, in which case one bottle will be enough for twelve guests.

– One bottle of alcohol (1 liter) yields approximately twenty-two drinks.

– One bottle of wine (750 ml) is enough for five glasses. Estimate one bottle for every three guests to be served during dinner. For the larger cocktail party where drinks will be a more popular choice, one bottle for every eight guests will be plenty. Also note white wine is usually more popular than red.

Tip!

Attach a unique ribbon around each glass's stem at your next cocktail party. This will allow your guests to recognize their glasses, even if they set them down for a minute while mingling. A nice touch and major dish saver!

Mix It Up!

- Jell-O Shots. You've seen them in every bad college movie. However, this tacky shot can be spruced up. Make Jell-O just like your mom used to but instead of adding water to the mixture, use alcohol. For example, serve lime-flavored Jell-O with gin on a slice of lime and you have a creation that tastes surprisingly similar to gin & tonic.

- Drink Recipes. You don't have to be a bartender to come up with your own drinks. Name your creation so it relates to your party theme. Remember to taste-test first. Not feeling that creative vibe? Simply rip off some old well-known recipes and rename them for the evening.

– Drinks for two. A hollowed-out coconut or a jumbo-sized milkshake glass is perfect for the single mingle. Put two straws in each glass and let the guests share.

– Chocolate. Decorate your glasses by dribbling melted chocolate on the inside of the glasses. Looks great and is edible too.

GET THE PARTY STARTED

*O*n the following pages you'll find recipes and tips that will help you throw fabulous parties. For a cocktail party, brunch, buffet, or dinner party, use these pages as a guide for suitable food, drink, and decorations. Don't be afraid to experiment and put your own personal touch on your events. That will make them stand out and fun to plan. The food recipes serve four people. Increase them proportionally if you have more guests. The bread recipes have a higher yield.

COCKTAIL PARTY

Starts between 5 PM and 8 PM
The classic "mingling" party.

MENU

Raspberry and Rose Martinis

Ginger Flavored Elderberry Martinis

Chocolate Truffle Martinis

French Fries with 3 Dips

Scandinavian Ceviche

Modern Cheese Tray

Mini Hamburgers with Foie Gras

Rosemary Skewers with Prosciutto and Monk Fish

Smoked Salmon Chips

Grapefruit and Campari Sorbet with
Mini Marshmallows

Truffled Mini Cupcakes

COCKTAIL PARTIES BECAME *trendy in the 1920s during prohibition. The economy was booming, and New York socialites tried to trump each other by throwing parties more lavish than one another. Because of prohibition, the events were hosted in private homes so they could sneak a drink now and then. As hostesses, women started to play a greater role in the social scene, which ultimately lead to it becoming acceptable for women to drink in the company of men. To this day, New York City is the cocktail capital of the world.*

DÉCOR

Sticking to your party theme is easy when arranging a cocktail party. An invitation connecting to your idea and decorative matching trays is pretty much all you need. If you want to go all out, you can decorate the space as well. Remember to place all your decorations at eye level, since the guests will be standing throughout the event. One larger flower arrangement in the middle of the room is always a safe bet. Hold the party in one room—a true cocktail party is always a bit crammed since it encourages mingling.

FOOD

The food served at a cocktail party is called hors d'oeuvres, which is essentially small finger food that your guests should be able to eat without a plate, in only a bite or two. Since the quantities of food are small, go for quality ingredients.

Hors d'oeuvres are divided into three categories: hot hors d'oeuvres, cold hors d'oeuvres, and canapés. What makes a canapé a canapé, and not a hors d'oeuvre, is that it has a flat and edible base, like an open-faced sandwich. Small squares of bread, crackers, or potato chips are all great bases for canapés. Traditionally at a cocktail party you are supposed to serve snacks from all three categories, and the more guests you have, the larger the variety of hors d'oeuvres there should be. Be creative when you plan your menu; any dish can be turned into a canapé or hors d'oeuvre. Your famous stew can be served in small hollowed-out puff pastry balls, or cut your favorite chocolate cake into small pieces and serve on a skewer together with a strawberry. Don't forget to always have at least one vegetarian alternative. Always serve more hearty alternatives in the beginning of the party and finish with lighter treats like dessert hors d'oeuvres.

SERVICE

Serve the hors d' oeuvres neatly, preferably in rows on trays. Make it more festive by using unexpected objects as your serving tray. Beautiful picture frames holding matching images, laminated record covers, bowls with oasis covered by moss to hold skewers in place, plexi glass, and exotic nontoxic leaves can be turned into excellent trays. Bowls holding dipping sauces or candles should be attached to the tray with double-sided tape or by placing a lemon slice underneath to avoid slips. Between servings, seltzer water is the best way to freshen up sticky trays.

Cocktail service is when the hostess and/or wait staff walk the room with serving trays. In the home, service is simplified by placing one cold hors d'oeuvres on a table so that guests can help themselves while you are working in the kitchen or working the room. In the absence of plates, you will need plenty of napkins. Hold the tray with one hand and a bundle of serviettes in the other one while serving. Put a plate stocked with napkins by the cold hors d'oeuvres table and tie a ribbon around them to make sure they stay put. Use smaller cocktail napkins, no bigger then 6 x 6 inches, and have four times as many as the amount of guests that are at your event, plus extras in the bar. Try to find serviettes that match your theme or personalize plain napkins by using stamps with cute motifs or your initials. Make sure there are drop tables where guests can put their used glasses and napkins.

DRINKS

Simplify by premixing drinks in pitchers well in advance; just wait to add the ice until right before your guests arrive. Stir, strain into garnished martini glasses, and serve on trays. All cocktails in this chapter can be easily prepared in advance. Generally two different types of cocktails for the evening is enough (for example, one with a gin base and another with vodka). By premixing, you save both time and cash since you decide the strength of the cocktails, and you don't have to stock up on supplies for a full bar.

The advantages of a bar, however, are that guests can mix their favorite drinks, and it can be a popular spot to gather, talk, swap drinks, and make new acquaintances. Either set up a DIY bar or ask a friend to play bartender. For instructions on how to set up your own bar, see the "Bar" chapter (p. 65-73).

Make sure you always have water and a nonalcoholic alternative available at the cocktail party. Beer is not generally served, but wine and/or champagne is perfectly acceptable. Individual mini champagne bottles served with a straw are a great bar-free alternative. Serve sweet dessert cocktails to signal the party has come to an end.

Tip!

State on the invitation when the party starts, but to avoid lingering guests, you can also add an ending time. A traditional cocktail party has at least twelve guests.

Hors d'oeuvre Facts

Tradition states that the more guests you invite, the more food alternatives you should serve.

Guests	Hors d'oeuvres
12–16	3–4 types minimum
17–25	4–5 types minimum
26+	5–6 types minimum

How Much Do People Eat?

Figure two of each type of hors d'oeuvres per guest if the party lasts a couple of hours. But take these factors into consideration:

* Timing. After work, guests will be hungry and eat more, so figure three of each type. If the party is held later in the evening, guests will already have eaten and the food will last longer.

* Cocktail hour. Are you planning on serving hors d'oeuvres followed by dinner? Figure about one of each type.

* Guests. Elderly people and women usually eat less, so consider your crowd when estimating your food.

RASPBERRY AND ROSE MARTINI

3 oz vodka
2 oz raspberry puree
1 oz raspberry liquor
Edible, non-toxic
    rose leaves

1. Wash the rose leaves thoroughly and mix with the vodka. Let the mixture sit overnight, or until you are ready to serve your drinks. Strain the flavored vodka.
2. Shake the puree and vodka in a cocktail shaker with ice and strain the drink into a martini glass.
3. Top the drink with raspberry liquor and decorate with a thoroughly cleaned rose leaf.

Tip!
Easily make your own raspberry puree by boiling equal parts sugar and water to make simple syrup (see page 72). Puree raspberries in a blender and add the simple syrup to taste. It's quick and a major flavor booster!

GINGER ELDERBERRY MARTINI

½ oz simple syrup
1 pinch dried and
    ground ginger
1 oz concentrated
    elderberry syrup
1 oz lime juice
3 oz gin
Lime wedge

1. Boil simple syrup (see page 72) and add the dried, ground ginger. Let the syrup cool to room temperature.
2. Add all the ingredients to a cocktail shaker with ice. Shake and strain into a martini glass.
3. Garnish with a lime wedge.

Tip!
In a hurry? Substitute ginger ale for simple syrup and ginger. If you want to add an extra twist to your cocktail, decorate the rim of the glass with a mixture of sugar and dried, ground ginger. Mix sugar and the ginger on a plate. Dampen the rim of the glass by swirling a lime wedge along the edge and then dip the glass in the sugar mixture. You can also simply decorate by adding a fruit flavored swirly stick—perfect if you want to serve the drink together with dessert.

Elderberry syrup can be found in well-stocked grocery stores and IKEA stores.

Tip!

All drink recipes yield one drink at a time using a cocktail shaker. If you are making cocktails for a crowd, then multiply and mix the ingredients in a pitcher. When the guests arrive simply add ice, stir, and strain into martini glasses. This might not be proper bar manners, but a big-time saver.

CHOCOLATE TRUFFLE MARTINI

2 oz Absolut mandarin
3 oz chocolate liquor
1 chocolate truffle
Orange peel

1. Burn orange peel over a martini glass (see page 73).
2. Mix the vodka and liquor with ice in a separate mixing glass. Stir well.
3. Place a chocolate truffle in the bottom of the cocktail glass with the citrus oil. Strain the beverage over the cocktail glass using a strainer.

Tip!
If you are serving a larger quantity of chocolate truffle martinis at the same time, it can be a chore to burn orange peel into each one. Instead, cut an orange peel into a spiral shape and serve in each glass. By cutting it in a spiral, more flavor will seep into the drink. You can also serve the drink with a rim of half unsweetened cacao power and half sugar. Swirl an orange wedge along the rim, and then dip the glass rim in the mixture.

Chocolate truffles can be bought in well-stocked grocery and specialty stores.

FRENCH FRIES WITH THREE DIPS

Serves 4 guests

4 large potatoes
1 tsp vegetable oil
Salt

1. Turn your oven to 425°F.
2. Peel the potatoes and cut them into equal sized sticks, about a ½ inch wide. Toss the pieces that are too small because they will burn in the oven.
3. Rinse the potatoes pieces and place them in a large pot of boiling salted water. Boil for 2 minutes. Strain the potatoes and rinse them in cold water until they cool. Place the potato sticks on a layer of paper towels and let them dry off.
4. Once dried, place the potatoes on a baking sheet lined with parchment paper. Dribble the oil on top and toss the potatoes with your hands until the oil is evenly distributed. Spread the potatoes evenly along the baking sheet, and make sure that the potato pieces are not touching each other.
5. Bake the potatoes in the middle of your oven for about 30 minutes. Turn the potatoes after about 15 minutes so they get even color.

Rosemary Mayonnaise

½ cup mayonnaise
2 tsp fresh chopped rosemary
Salt and pepper to taste

1. Mix the mayo and rosemary.
2. Let it sit for at least an hour in the fridge. When you are ready to serve the sauce, add salt and pepper to taste.

Wasabi Mustard

2 tbsp of Dijon mustard
4 tbsp of crème fraiche
½ tsp of wasabi
Salt and white pepper to taste

1. Mix the mustard and crème fraiche in a bowl and add the wasabi. Start with ¼ tsp and taste the mixture. Then add the rest to desired spiciness. Keep in mind that the flavor will be enhanced the longer the dipping sauce sits.
2. Let the mixture sit for at least an hour in the fridge. When you are ready to serve the sauce, add salt and pepper to taste.

Curry Ketchup

½ cup ketchup
2 tsp curry

1. Mix the ketchup and curry, and let it sit for at least an hour in the fridge.

Serving tip: Nothing says "party" like individual serving cups—they are easy for your guests to hold while mingling and look great. Serve the fries in decorative cones made out of any decorative paper or even something simple like a newspaper (why not the yellow pages?). Roll the paper into proportionate cones, line them with wax paper, and staple them at the edge. Serve the cones on a tray with the dipping sauces. Make the perfect tray yourself by punching holes in a box lid and placing the cones in the holes.

Simplify: Buy frozen French fries from your grocery store that just need to be heated or even ready-made ones from a restaurant. Get rid of the "evidence" and serve the fries in decorative cones with your homemade sauces.

For a challenge: Chop fresh herbs and mix with the pommes when they come out of the oven. It looks, smells, and tastes great. You can also use different colored potatoes, such as red skinned, orange sweet potatoes, or blue potatoes of the delta blue variety.

SCANDINAVIAN CEVICHE

Serves 4 guests

1 grapefruit
½ avocado
4 ounces pre sliced gravlax (or smoked salmon)
2 tbsp finely diced red onion

1. Fillet the grapefruit by first cutting off the peel so that the citrus flesh is exposed. Then cut out the fillets by angling the knife and cutting by the natural partings. The fillets come out in half moon shapes. Cut the fillets into ½ inch pieces.
2. Peel and chop the red onion coarsely. Peel the avocado and cut into ½ inch cubes. Do the same with the salmon slices.
3. Mix all the ingredients in a plastic bowl or plastic bag. Let the mixture soak for at least an hour in the fridge.

Serving tip!
Serve the ceviche in shot glasses with a teaspoon. Ceviche tastes best cool, so serve the shot glasses on a deep tray filled with ice.

Simplify:
This dish keeps well in the refrigerator and can be prepared up to twenty-four hours beforehand; the citrus juice ensures the avocado doesn't turn brown and dull.

For a challenge:
Make a more traditional ceviche by using raw fish, shrimp, or scallops. Use lime juice instead of grapefruit, and add chopped tomatoes and cilantro. Use white fish, such as cod or snapper. Always freeze the fish for at least 3 days before you use it to kill any possible parasites.

MODERN CHEESE TRAY

3 oz assorted cheeses per
person

Think a cheese tray sounds horribly dated and brings back memories from your mother's old parties? Think again: the taste variations are endless. Cheese is usually produced from goat's, sheep's, water buffalo's, or cow's milk. A cheese produced by the same method, with the same type of milk, will taste completely different depending on where in the world it is produced. Choose cheeses with different firmness, made with different milks, and from different countries. Don't forget artisnal American cheeses are world class.

Serving tip!
Serve the cheese at room temperature to enhance the flavor, together with bread, fruit, and homemade marmalades and compotes. Place the cheese tray on a table and leave it there throughout the party so your guests always have access.

Simplify:
Ask for help at your grocery store's cheese counter or in the dairy department if you feel unsure about what varieties to pick. They will happily help you choose an interesting mix. Buy ready-made marmalades or jams, and just heat up.

For a Challenge:
Homemade bread is a perfect compliment. Try the recipe on p.131.

Apricot and Chili Marmalade

Serves 4 guests

6 oz good quality apricot
marmalade
2 tsp chili flakes

1. Heat up the marmalade and chili flakes over low heat. Make sure it doesn't boil. Taste it; the mixture should have a light, hot aftertaste.
2. Serve warm.

Truffle Honey

6 oz honey
3 tbsp of truffle oil
Salt and pepper to taste

1. Lightly heat up the honey so that it melts. Add the truffle oil, and salt and pepper to taste.
2. Let it cool down and serve at room temperature.

Port Wine Poached Dates

¼ cup port wine
½ cup dates
Pepper to taste

1. Chop the dates roughly. Add to a sauce pan, and add the port wine. Bring to a simmer over low heat for 15 minutes or until the sauce has thickened.
2. Pepper to taste.

CHEESE TERMINOLOGY
– Show off at the cheese counter

Fromage—French for cheese

Cendre—French for cheese that has ripened in ash

Pecorino—Italian for cheese made with sheep's milk

Ferme/Fermier—French for cheese produced on a farm

Coulant—French for runny cheeses such as a Brie or Camembert

Capra—Italian for goat's milk cheese

Chèvr—the French word for goat, used to describe all goat's milk cheeses

Bleu—the French word for blue, used to describe blue cheese/blue vein cheese

Tome—French word used to describe cheeses produced in the mountain regions

QUICK GUIDE TO IMPORTED CHEESES

FRESH OR UNRIPENED CHEESE
Feta—Greek sheep's or goat's milk cheese, salted

Mascarpone—cheese from Italy, made with cow's milk and commonly used for desserts since it has a sweet flavor

Mozzarella—cheese from Italy, traditionally made with water buffalo's milk, also has a sweet flavor

Ricotta—cheese from Italy, consistency similar to cottage cheese, traditionally used in pasta sauces

SOFT CHEESE
Cheeses with a thin skin and a creamy center

Brie—French rind ripened cheese made from cow's milk

Camembert—French rind ripened cheese, made with cow's milk similar to Brie but with a slightly milder flavor

Boursin—French triple cream cow's milk cheese, usually flavored with spices and herbs

SEMI-SOFT CHEESE
Soft and sliceable texture

Fontina—Italian cow's milk cheese

Gorgonzola—the famous blue vein Italian cow's milk cheese, which is much creamier then Stilton or Roquefort

Havarti—Danish cow's milk cheese, often flavored with dill

Gouda—Dutch cheese with a red or yellow wax, made from cow's milk and has a creamy texture

Roquefort—French blue vein cheese, made with sheep's milk

Stilton—British blue vein cheese made from cow's milk.

FIRM CHEESE
Cheddar—the world's most famous cheese is a cow's milk cheese produced both in Great Britain and the United States. It is naturally white, but is sometimes dyed orange. Tastes best when made from raw milk and aged.

Emmenthale—Swiss cow's milk cheese

Gruyère—Swiss cow's milk cheese, that is similar in taste to Emmenthaler, but is aged longer and has a stronger flavor.

Provolone—flavorful Italian cheese, made from cow's milk. Dolce is aged for 2 months, Piccante for 6 months. It also comes smoked.

HARD CHEESE
Aged and usually very flavorful

Asiago—Italian flavorful cow's milk cheese that is aged for at least 2 years

Parmigiano—Reggiano (Parmesan) Italian cow's milk cheese, made exclusively in the region near Parma. One of the world's oldest and most copied cheeses.

Percorino-Romano—Italian sheep's milk cheese from southern Italy.

Cheesy Trends

These days cheese has become a hot topic among foodies. Chefs are going on cheese trips instead of wine tastings, and people are leaving their 9 to 5 jobs to become "apprentices" at tiny cheese farms in the country and dedicating their lives to producing fifty cheeses a year. Why not arrange your own cheese tasting? Invite your friends over and ask them each to buy one cheese and to learn a little about it for the evening so they can share their knowledge with everyone.

Tip!

– Spanish cheeses are usually of the finest quality and taste, but are overshadowed by their famous French competition. Usually you can get a great-tasting Spanish cheese for a lot cheaper then a French one.

– Cheese can be paired with anything from beer to cider, but most still prefer wine. A rule of thumb: when pairing the two together, pick cheeses and wines from the same region.

MINI HAMBURGERS WITH FOIE GRAS

Serves 4 guests

4 oz of good quality ground
    beef (10 percent fat max)
4 mini-hamburger buns
4 tsp mayonnaise
1 oz foie gras of 4 thin slices
Salt and pepper

1. Set your oven to broil. Split the ground beef into 4 equal parts and shape them into mini-burger patties. Salt and pepper them well on both sides.
2. Place the patties on a baking sheet lined with parchment paper and broil them high up in the oven for a total of approximately 6 minutes, 3 minutes on each side.
3. Split the mini-hamburger buns, and place them in the oven the last minute so that they become warm and slightly toasted.
4. Add mayonnaise and pepper on the inside of the buns, place the beef patty on top of the bottom part, and then add the slice of foie gras. This way it will melt slightly. Top it with the other bun and spear a toothpick through to keep everything in place.

Simplify:
If you are having a hard time finding mini-hamburger buns, use mini-potato rolls, brioche, toast, or simply split a regular size bun in half. You can also substitute foie gras for duck or goose liver pate.

For a challenge:
Instead of a regular toothpick, use a Japanese skewer with a little stylish knot on top. Add a little cognac and a touch of cayenne to the mayonnaise to add another dimension of flavor. For the best flavor boost, buy sirloin and grind it in your food processor for about fifteen seconds to make your own beef patties.

Foie Gras isn't exactly politically correct, but it is delicious. It is made from goose or duck liver from a bird that has been force fed to get an extra fatty liver. (The word foie gras literally means fatty liver.) Foie gras isn't commonly used in American cooking, but it's a classic hors d'oeuvre ingredient. It comes in metal cans similar to spam and stores almost as long, so if you happen to be passing through France, pick some up.

ROSEMARY SKEWERS WITH PROSCIUTTO AND MONK FISH

Serves 4 guests

12 oz monk fish, cod or other
    white firm fish
4 rosemary spruces
4 slices of prosciutto ham
Salt and pepper

1. Cut the fish in 1 inch square pieces. Salt and pepper them lightly.
2. Rinse the rosemary spruces and cut them to about 5 inch long skewers. Clean off the leaves, leaving only a few at the top.
3. Skewer the fish pieces onto the rosemary skewer, and wrap the ham around the fish.
4. Grill the skewer in the oven with your broiler at 425°F for 4 minutes per side. Serve the skewers hot out of the oven.

½ tbs grated lemon zest
2 tbs lemon juice
2 tbs coarsely chopped shallots
1 tsp butter
5 tbs crème fraiche (or sour
    cream)
Salt and white pepper

Citrus creme

1. Wash the lemons well in warm water and zest the peel on a grater, without getting any of the bitter white part. Squeeze the lemon juice. Peel and coarsely chop the shallots.
2. Melt the butter in a small saucepan. Once the butter is hot and stops bubbling, add the shallots and sauté them until they become translucent. Add the lemon zest, followed by the juice.
3. Take the pan off the heat, and stir in the crème fraiche. Salt and pepper to taste.
4. Pour the sauce into 4 small shot glasses or decorative cups, and serve the skewers on top.

Serving tip!
By serving the skewers on top of, or in, the sauce cup, your guests can walk around and mingle while eating. They can also avoid drips and the dreaded double-dip.

Simplify:
The rosemary skewers can be prepared up to twenty-four hours beforehand, and will taste better after resting and absorbing the rosemary flavor. Just pop them in the oven when the guests arrive.

For a challenge:
The fish absorbs the flavor of the rosemary, so the herb works both as spice and skewer. Test out other herb skewers, such as thyme or sage. To get a different flavor for the sauce, try using Moroccan preserved lemon peel instead of fresh lemon. It adds an exotic salty/sour flavor.

SMOKED SALMON CHIPS

Serves 4 guests

6 slices of smoked salmon
12 large potato chips
2 tbs crème fraiche (or sour
  cream)
Chive, thyme or dill for
  decoration

1. Divide each salmon slice in two, roll them to an appropriate size, and place them on the chips.
2. Put the crème fraich in a plastic bag and cut a little hole in one corner to make the bag work as a piping bag. Pipe about ½ tsp onto each salmon chip.
3. Decorate with chive, thyme, or dill.

Simplify:
Make it easy on yourself by placing all the ingredients on a tray and letting your guests compose their own hors d'oeuvres.

For a challenge:
Spice it up by using different types of chips such as sweet potato, delta blue potato, or daikon radish. Works well with caviar instead of salmon, too. You can also make your own chips in the oven with thin slices of potatoes.

GRAPEFRUIT AND CAMPARI SORBET WITH MINI MARSHMALLOWS

Serves 4 guests

2 limes
4 scoops of grapefruit sorbet
4 tbs Campari
⅛ cup mini marshmallows

1. Cut a thin sliver of peel at both ends of the limes. This will create a smooth bottom so they can stand securely. Split the lime in half, and remove all the flesh with a teaspoon or melon scooper. Place the emptied lime halves in the freezer for at least an hour.
2. Use a melon scooper or tablespoon to scoop the sorbet into a size that will fit in the lime halves. Place a scoop in each lime and place in the freezer until serving time.
3. When ready to serve, pour a tablespoon of Campari over each scoop, and garnish with mini marshmallows. Serve with a teaspoon and cocktail napkin.

Simplify:
Campari is a bitter tasting aperitif from Italy, has a strong red color, and is usually served with soda. It might not be something you have at home, but it's worth a try. You can also try other combinations such as orange sorbet with port wine, or lemon sorbet with Limoncello or ice wine.

For a challenge:
If you happen to have an ice-cream maker at home, break it out of storage and try making your own sorbet. It's a lot easier and quicker then making ice cream and tastes great.

BRUNCH

Starts between 11 AM and 1 PM
Casual, easy, and a time saver.

MENU

Wasabi Bloody Mary

Valencia Mimosa

–

Banana Bread with Honey Butter

Chive Waffles with Horseradish Cream

Salmon with Orange and Herb Sauce

Spinach and Asparagus Salad With Poached Eggs

–

Yogurt Rice Pudding with Grilled Fruit Skewers

BRUNCH IS, *just as it sounds, a combination of breakfast and lunch. The phenomenon was invented at the end of the 19th century when the British upper class started serving a large breakfast after their morning hunt. The French socialites didn't want to miss out and actually started hosting hunting parties where servants arranged extravagant hunting picnics, including over-the-top decorations such as chandeliers in the trees. But it wasn't until the 1930s that Hollywood put brunch on the map. During that time, the movie stars frequently traveled by train between LA and NYC. In Chicago, you had to change trains, and the celebrities used the opportunity to have a big, lunch-like breakfast in the "Pump Room" at the world famous Ambassador Hotel. They ate, cheek-kissed, and networked. And all of a sudden, everyone wanted to do "brunch."*

DÉCOR

Decorate your brunch according to your theme, but think quality. Bring out your best china, and skip the stapling, taping, and cheating you can get away with at an evening party, as daylight will expose any flaws. Brunch works well the morning after you've hosted a large event with many out-of-towners, like a bridal shower, bachelorette party, or engagement party. While eating, you get a chance to chat and gossip about the previous night, and it makes the travelers feel extra appreciated. Brunch can also kick-off a day together with friends. Catch up while enjoying your homemade creations, and then hit that shopping spree, pilates class, or planned museum visit. Match the theme with the planned activity.

> ### Tip!
> Crazy schedule? Brunch is the perfect party. Quick, easy, and over by 2 PM. Once you have kissed your guests good-bye, you still have plenty of time to run all your errands and plan other activities. Save the dishes for later!

FOOD

Your guests will arrive hungry since it is the first meal of the day. So sit down at the table as soon as everyone has arrived and don't be stingy with the portions. Just like the name suggests, the food served should be a fusion between breakfast and lunch, with the emphasis on lunch. (If your guests have been hitting the clubs the night before, keep that in mind when planning your menu since they probably will be craving a heavier meal.) Considering brunch's Anglo-Saxon origin, most connect it with food such as sausages, bacon, pancakes, and scrambled eggs, but there are no rules. Serve what you think fits your theme and guests. For a spa-brunch, you might toast your own muesli and serve together with lychee and lime yogurt, multi-grain toast, and a fresh-squeezed juice bar. Unless you are a natural early bird, preparing as much as possible of your menu the night before is the key to a no-sweat brunch party.

SERVICE

Brunch is a relaxed affair commonly hosted during the weekend when guests' schedules allow. You can choose either to serve it as a buffet or seated meal. If you are serving it seated, then set your table after traditional dinner guidelines (see "table setting," p.51–63). Buffet style is the most common way to serve brunch. (See "Buffet," p. 124 for set up details.) If you have a large dining table, you can conveniently combine the two serving styles. Set half the table dinner style, and use the other half to set up your buffet. This way you can seat and serve your guests at the same table. Use two tablecloths to differentiate the sides. A traditional brunch is a small, seated, and intimate affair served at a single table, but it is diverse enough to work for most event sizes. Host a brunch birthday bash, or even a brunch the day after a wedding for out-of-towners and close family. Don't forget, always have seating for everyone.

DRINKS

Your guests will come for the food, but they'll stay for the drinks. Because what's a brunch without a few Bloody Marys and mimosas? Both drinks originated in France and have been around for more than eighty years. The bubbly Mimosa is said to have first been mixed in the luxurious Ritz Hotel, Paris, 1952. Bloody Marys first saw daylight in the same city just after World War I when the French started to import tomato juice from America. Originally the drink was mixed using gin, but in the 1960s, Smirnoff started using the drink in their marketing campaigns, and it became a vodka based drink. Today the Bloody Mary has claimed its fame as the ultimate "morning after" drink. Compliment your drink selection with tea, coffee, and fresh juices at the brunch.

WASABI BLOODY MARY

1 oz vodka
2 dashes of Worcestershire
sauce
2 dashes of Tabasco
¼ oz lemon juice
Pinch of wasabi on tub
4 oz tomato juice
Salt and pepper
Lemon slice
Cocktail tomato

1. Mix the sauces, wasabi, and juice. Stir well and flavor with salt and pepper to taste.
2. Fill the serving glass halfway with ice, and add the vodka and juice mixture. Stir well.
3. Decorate with a lemon slice and cocktail tomato on a skewer.

Tip!
Prepare the juice mixture well in advance. It makes your brunch easier to prepare in the morning, and the flavor is enhanced from letting the mixture sit.

VALENCIA MIMOSA

2 oz fresh orange juice
1 oz apricot liquor
4 oz champagne or sparkling
wine

1. First pour the orange juice in the champagne glasses and then add the champagne. To avoid losing the bubbles, don't stir, but pull the juice up along the sides with a spoon.
2. Top with the apricot liquor.

BANANA BREAD WITH HONEY BUTTER

Serves 4 guests

3 well-ripened bananas
3 oz butter
½ cup sugar
2 eggs
1½ cup flour
½ cup muesli
½ tsp salt
1 tsp vanilla extract
2 tsp baking powder
3 tbsp brown sugar

1. Turn your oven to 350°F. Peel the bananas and use a fork to crush two of them. Slice the third one.
2. Melt the butter. Beat the sugar and eggs until fluffy and white. Once the butter has cooled, add it to the egg mixture.
3. Mix the flour, baking powder, and salt in a separate bowl. Slowly add the flour mix to the egg mix, and then do the same with the crushed bananas.
4. Butter and flour a cake pan, approximately 5 x 8 inch. Pour the batter into the pan, and top it with the sliced banana and brown sugar.
5. Bake in the middle of the oven for 25–30 minutes. Check the bread with a toothpick. If it is dry, the bread is ready.

Honey Butter

4 oz butter
4 tbsp honey
1 tsp coarse salt

1. Leave the butter out and let it reach room temperature. This takes about an hour.
2. Stir the butter and drizzle the honey, mixing it slightly so it creates a layered effect. Add the salt on top.

Simplify:
You can mix the batter the day before, and store it in the baking pan ready to pop in the oven. It's important to keep the batter cool as you are preparing it, and store it in the refrigerator so the baking powder does not begin to rise.

For a challenge:
To make healthier bread, you can experiment with different types of flour. You can also add less flour and more muesli, as well as walnuts, etc.

CHIVE WAFFLES WITH HORSERADISH CREAM

Serves 4 guests

5 oz butter
1 cup flour
½ cup whole wheat flour
2 tsp baking powder
1 tsp salt
5 tbsp chopped chives
1 cup milk
1 cup water

½ cup of heavy whipping
   cream
2 tbsp of grated horse
   radish
salt and white pepper

1. Clean and heat a waffle iron. Melt the butter.
2. Mix all the dry ingredients and add the chopped chives. Add the milk, water, and finally the melted butter. The consistency should be thick.
3. Brush the waffle iron with a little melted butter before you add the batter. Add an appropriate amount of batter depending on the size of your iron. Let the waffle cook until golden and crispy.

Horseradish Cream

1. Whip the cream until stiff peaks are created, and then add the horseradish. Salt and pepper to taste.

Simplify:
When serving multiple guests it can be time consuming to bake the waffles and keep them warm until serving. Create a waffle station where the guests can make their own waffles. It's fun and social for the guests, and you can enjoy a mimosa instead.

For a challenge:
This savory waffle recipe can replace toast on your brunch menu and goes well with salmon. You can also experiment with different waffle batters and let your guests pick their own favorites. Make a sweet batter by adding vanilla flavor, or try one with spinach and lemon peel.

SALMON WITH ORANGE AND HERB SAUCE

Serves 4 guests

1 pound of salmon fillet
parchment paper
3 oz of butter
2 tbsp lemon zest
2 oz leaks
3 oz fennel
2 oz carrots
2 oz celery
1 egg
Salt and pepper to taste

1. Turn your oven to 425°F. Split the salmon into four equal-size portions. Cut the parchment paper into four heart shapes. The hearts should be large enough to wrap the salmon pieces.
2. Melt ¼ of the butter. Mix the remaining butter with salt, pepper, and lemon zest to taste.
3. Wash and peel the vegetables. Cut them julienne style, which means even and extremely thin sticks.
4. Brush one side of the heart shapes with the melted butter, and place the julienne vegetables on the brushed papers.
5. Place the salmon on top of the vegetables, and a ¼ of the butter mixture on top of the salmon. Wrap the second part of the heart over the salmon, and fold in the ends so it forms a package that holds tight. Beat the egg in a cup using a fork, and brush the parchment paper with the egg. This will help it stick together.
6. Place the salmon packets on a sheet pan, and bake in the middle of the oven for 8–10 minutes. The packets should be golden brown and puff up in the oven.

Orange and Fresh Herb Sauce

2 cups fresh orange juice
⅛ vegetable bullion cube
2 tbs chopped fresh herb,
such as parsley, thyme, and
marjoram
2 tbs chopped fresh chives
3 tbs butter
White pepper to taste

1. Bring the orange juice and bullion to a boil in a small saucepan. Let it reduce by simmering over medium heat without a lid for 20 minutes.
2. When reduced, add the fresh herbs, chives, and pepper to taste.
3. Remove the pot from the heat and add the butter. Stir until the butter has melted and the sauce has a glossy finish.

Serving tip!
Serve the individual packet to each guest. This will also keep the fish warm until serving time. Great with the savory waffles and horseradish cream.

Simplify:
You can save time by making one large salmon packet, or even buying smoked salmon that you serve with the orange sauce.

For a challenge:
If you're feeling really ambitious, pan smoke your own salmon in a pan with wood chips.

SPINACH AND ASPARAGUS SALAD WITH POACHED EGGS

Serves 4 guests

¾ lb fresh baby spinach
10 red pearl onions—can
    be substituted with 1
    chopped red onion
1 bunch of asparagus
1 tbsp butter
4 tbsp olive oil
4 tbsp lemon juice
Salt and pepper to taste

1. Wash and clean the baby spinach. Dry it completely in a salad spinner or using paper towels. Place in your salad bowl.
2. Peel and cut the onions and add to the spinach.
3. Clean and break off the lower part of the asparagus. Cut it into smaller pieces.
4. Add the butter to a frying pan. Once hot, add the asparagus and sauté for about four minutes.
5. Take the pan off the heat, and add the olive oil and lemon juices. Salt and pepper to taste, and then add the asparagus. Pour pan's contents on top of the salad.

Tip!
The bottom part of the asparagus stem is hard and should be removed before serving. To know exactly where to cut it off, break each asparagus by holding each end and letting it snap on its own. It will natural break off at the right part.

Poached Eggs

2 tsp salt
2 tsp vinegar
4 eggs

1. Fill a large pot halfway with water and bring it to a boil. Add the salt and vinegar, and reduce the heat to a simmer.
2. Carefully break one egg into a cup. Make sure that the yolk does not break. Slowly and carefully add the egg to the simmering water, and then repeat the procedure with the rest of the eggs.
3. Let the eggs simmer for 3–5 minutes, depending on how runny you like them. Serve them directly over the salad or put them in an ice bath for later serving.

Serving tip!
Serve the eggs in individual ramekins. It looks very festive and the eggs keep warm longer.

Simplify:
An easy time saver is to clean and cut the asparagus and spinach the day before. Keep it in a bowl filled with water until you are ready to make the salad.

For a challenge:
You can always add other vegetables to the salad. Just like the waffles, this works great with salmon.

YOGURT RICE PUDDING WITH GRILLED FRUIT SKEWERS

Serves 4 guests

2 portions of risotto rice
½ cup whipping cream
½ cup of plain yogurt
3 tbsp sugar
1 tsp vanilla extract

1. Follow the instructions on the risotto rice package to make two portions of boiled rice. Exclude the salt. Let the rice cool in a bowl in the refrigerator.
2. When you are ready to serve, whip the cream and sugar until it creates stiff peaks. Add the yogurt and the vanilla extract.
3. Mix the creamy mixture with the cooled rice.

Fruit of your choice
For example: pineapple, peach, plums, mango, pears, strawberries, etc.

Fruit Skewers

1. Clean and cut the fruit into ½ inch cubes. Add the fruit to small wooden skewers. To enhance the flavor of the fruit, quickly grill the skewers for a minute in a grill pan or oven with a broil function.

Serving tip!
Serve the rice pudding in small bowls or drinking glasses. Add a skewer to each bowl and grate some nutmeg over each. A trick when serving skewers is to place half a mango or other fruit on the serving tray so the guests have somewhere to discard their used skewers. That way you get an easy clean-up.

Simplify:
Boil the rice the day before, and mix in the yogurt, vanilla, and sugar. When you are ready to serve, whip the cream and add it to the mix.

For a challenge:
Mix ¼ cup of raisins with 3 tbsp of spicy dark rum. Let the raisins swell and absorb the rum overnight. Add the rum/raisin mix to the pudding for a sweet flavor enhancer.

BUFFET

Buffets can be hosted both during the day and night. This hearty menu is more suitable for an evening affair, starting between 6:00 — 9:00 PM.

MENU

Lavender and Peach Bellini

—

Salt Crusted Walnut Bread

Chèvre with Candied Figs

Wild Mushroom and Lemon Risotto

Tarragon Chicken with Anchovy Cream

Lamb Skewers with Hot Pistachio and Mint Sauce

Tomato and Arugula Salad with Balsamic Bacon

—

Spice Crusted Chocolate Tart with
Pineapple and Pink Peppercorn Compote

IT'S A TRIED *and true tradition to let guests serve themselves from a buffet. In the Middle Ages, banquets were the party style du jour. In 18th-century France, the modern buffet was developed and its popularity quickly spread across Europe. Until the early 20th century, it was strictly forbidden to serve any buffet dishes that required the use of a knife. The idea was that the guests should be able to eat while standing, with the plate in one hand and the fork in the other. Today seating at a buffet is common, and it is therefore acceptable to serve food that requires cutting.*

DÉCOR

The buffet table generally becomes the focus of the room, so spend time decorating it. The first step is to make sure it's well lit, but be conservative with candles since guests can easily burn themselves when stretching over the buffet to fill their plates. It is also a fire hazard, and flaming buffets are not a hit (been there, done that!). Use smart design and simple decorations to impress your guests. Write and frame cards explaining each dish and ingredient to place next to the courses. Wrap the cutlery in napkins, tying ribbons to hold the sets together. This looks nice and at the same time makes it simple for the guests to carry. Place food on different levels for a great visual effect, but also for easy access. Keep in mind that higher objects catch the eye first, so spend extra time on the presentations for the top level serving trays.

FOOD

On average, each guest will eat one pound of food from the buffet. Dishes on the light side are more popular than heavy ones. When planning your buffet pick dishes that will taste good at room temperature. Fifteen to twenty percent of the buffet served should be vegetarian. Hot food can be tricky; serve it in smaller amounts and have the serving plates changed frequently. If you are starting to run out of a dish, or simply don't have that much, place it toward the end of the buffet. When the guests reach the dish their plates will already be filled, and they won't take as much.

SERVICE

At a buffet guests serve themselves. Therefore it's not considered a very posh way to throw an event. However, guests appreciate the ability to pick their own foods and as the host or hostess, it is the best way to serve a crowd swiftly. You can either serve a buffet standing or seated. A standing buffet accommodates more guests in a smaller space and requires less preparation. For a seated buffet, you can either set the tables with cutlery, napkins, and glasses—as for a regular dinner party—or you can place the tools on the buffet table and let your guests pick it up themselves. Set up the buffet table close to the kitchen to avoid the crowd when replenishing the serving plates. When a serving plate is half-empty, exchange it for a new one. The exception is during a rush. Then you can let the plates empty completely before you bring out a new one. If your buffet party is a larger event, plan on having two extra plates with food prepped in the kitchen from the start: one plate filled with food ready for serving, and the other half-full. Swap the serving plate on the buffet for the full plate when it is half-finished. In the kitchen, transfer the leftovers from the buffet serving plate to the new, half-full, plate. Serving utensils should be placed on small plates lined with a napkin in front of each respective dish. If you want to be fancy, use tongs for your bread. A modern buffet trend is to use TV-dinner plates with separate compartments for each dish. It's so ugly it looks cool, and the guests avoid having the stew touch their shrimp salad.

BUFFET TYPES

One-Sided Buffet

Set up your buffet table against a wall so that the food is served only from one side. This works great for a normal-sized buffet, hosted in the home. When space is tight, use a round table placed in the middle of the room for your buffet.

Double-Sided Buffet

When hosting a bigger party, serve a double-sided buffet to avoid lines. Place the table so that the guests can approach from both sides and have utensils on both sides.

Stations

Split up the buffet by setting up food stations throughout the space. One station for courses served at room temperature, one for hot food, and a separate dessert station. This option helps you accommodate large groups, creates a good flow in the space, or spreads out guests if the venue is big.

DRINKS

Before the guests indulge in your buffet, it's nice to treat them to a tasty and welcoming drink. The classy Bellini cocktail was invented in 1948 by Giuseppe Cipriani at Harry's Bar in Venice, Italy. The original version is made with white peach purée, a rare fruit that is ripe for only four months out of the year. The Bellini became popular in the States when the Cipriani restaurant empire set up shop in New York. The buffet in this book highlights Italian flavors, so the Bellini is a perfect starter. For the buffet, feel free to place wine and beverages directly on the dinner table. Another option is to set up a separate beverage station for wine, water, nonalcoholic alternatives, and glasses.

How Much Will Your Guest Eat?

Meat, bird, or fish	6 oz
Potato, rice, pasta, bread	5 oz
Vegetables	5 oz
Total	16 oz

In the Right Order

To ensure that the buffet runs smoothly, organize it as follows:

1. Plates
2. Salads and dressings
3. Smaller dishes and their sides
4. Main courses and their sides
5. Bread
6. Butter, salt, pepper
7. Cutlery and glasses

LAVENDER AND PEACH BELLINI

1 part peach puree
2 parts Prosecco or another
sparkling wine
1 pinch of edible, nontoxic,
dried or fresh lavender

1. Place the puree in the bottom of a champagne glass.
2. Carefully pour in the sparkling wine.
3. Don't stir, but use a spoon to pull the puree up along the sides of the glass, so that you wont lose the bubbles.
4. Decorate with the lavender.

Tip!
If you are having a hard time finding peach puree, you can also use high quality peach juice or another fruit puree. A classic Bellini has peach liquor as a top layer.

SALT CRUSTED WALNUT BREAD

¼ oz bag of yeast
2 cups lukewarm water
2 tsp salt
2 tbsp honey
½ cup olive oil
½ cup peeled walnuts
5 cups flour
Sea salt

1. In a large mixing bowl or Kitchen Aid, add the yeast, lukewarm water, salt, honey, and ¾ of the olive oil. Stir and let the yeast dissolve.
2. Roughly chop the walnuts, and mix in the batter together with the flour. Add a little at a time, while mixing in a processor for 5 minutes, or by hand for 10 minutes. It should have a loose consistency when done.
3. Let the dough rise, under a tea towel in a warm nondrafty place until it has doubled in size.
4. Puncture the dough with a fork so the air goes out of it. Let it rise to double the size a second time, and puncture again. Wash and flour your hands, and place the dough onto a sheet pan lined with parchment paper. Shape it into a ball.
5. Turn your oven to 475°F.
6. Let the dough rise a third time to double the size on the sheet pan covered with a tea towel.
7. Brush the dough with the remaining olive oil and add a few teaspoons of sea salt to the top.
8. Place the bread in the middle of the oven for approximately 15 minutes. Lower the temp to 300°F and let it bake for an additional 40 minutes.

Serving tip!

You can skip the butter with this bread, since it has an olive oil and salted crust. It works well served with cheese on the buffet.

Simplify:

Home baked bread is a great addition to any meal, but if you're in a pinch just buy ready-made nut bread at the baker, and dampen the crust. Heat in the oven for 5 minutes for a fresh taste.

For a challenge:

Individual portions are always a crowd pleaser. Make rolls from the same recipe, and while you're at it, freeze a few for other occasions. Save for up to three months in the freezer.

CHÈVRE WITH CANDIED FIGS

Serves 4 guests

¾ pound chèvre or other
    goat cheese
4 fresh figs or ½ cup dried
¼ cup of balsamic vinegar
3 tbsp of brown muscovado
    sugar, or brown sugar

1. Slice the chèvre log, and place on an oven pan. Cut the figs into rounds.
2. Pour the balsamic vinegar and sugar into a small pot, and bring it to a boil. Lower the heat and let it simmer until the mixture is reduced and sticks to the back of a spoon.
3. If you are using dried figs, place them in the vinegar mixture and let them absorb some of the fluid while the mixture cools.
4. Heat the chèvre cheese slices quickly by using your oven's broiler function for about 3 minutes, or until the cheese has slightly started to melt. Place the cheese on a serving plate, and top it with the candied figs and vinegar mixture. Serve warm.

Simplify:
You can replace muscavado sugar with brown sugar, honey, or regular sugar. Always taste the mixture since the different sugars have different sweetness, and you might have to add more.

For a challenge:
With their peppery honey flavor, Black Mission figs are the best money can buy. Fresh Black Mission figs are only available a few weeks out of the year, so if you happen to come across some, make compotes and freeze for later use.

Muscovado sugar
The sugar is available in light and dark flavors, and is a raw sugar made from sugar canes. Compared with regular refined sugar, it is less processed and high in mineral content. The darker sugar has a liquorish flavor, and the lighter version has a toffee flavor.

WILD MUSHROOM AND LEMON RISOTTO

Serves 4 guests

½ cup of dried mixed wild
  mushrooms
4 cups of chicken or
  vegetable stock
2 large shallots
2 tbsp olive oil
1 cup of risotto rice, for
  example Arborio
⅓ cup white wine
¼ cup heavy cream
¼ cup grated parmesan
  cheese
2 tbsp lemon zest
Salt and pepper to taste

1. Place the dried mushrooms in a small sauce pan, and add water until the mushrooms are just barely covered. Bring it to a boil, then remove the pot from the heat and let it steep for one hour. After an hour, strain the mushrooms but keep the water, and add it to the stock for flavor.
2. Heat the stock. Peel and finely chop the shallots. Roughly chop the mushrooms.
3. In a large heavy bottom pan, heat the olive oil. Add the shallots, mushrooms, and rice and let it sauté on medium heat until the rice is translucent in color.
4. Add the wine to the mixture. Stir with a wooden spoon until most of the fluid has been absorbed, and it has a porridgelike consistency.
5. Add the stock, ¼ cup at a time. Boil at medium heat and stir constantly until most of the stock has been absorbed. Repeat until all the stock has been added. This should take about 20 minutes.
6. When the rice is al dente it's ready to be served. Add the cream, parmesan cheese, mushrooms, and lemon zest. Salt and pepper to taste.

Serving tip!
Serve the risotto either straight out of the pan or in large hollowed-out cheese balls. Serving out of cheese is a fun alternative and also adds flavor to the risotto when it melts. Choose a hard flavorful cheese such as manchego or parmesan. The cheese balls are also a nice addition on the buffet to go with the walnut bread.

Simplify:
Risotto is simple, can be varied a million different ways, and is a great buffet dish. It should be prepared close to serving time. Even though simple to make, risotto does demand a lot of attention and needs to be stirred. Recruit a friend to stir while you prepare the rest of the buffet. In case of an emergency, you can prepare it in advance and place under foil in the oven. Just add a little more cream right before serving.

For a challenge:
The stock, not the wine, is what makes the risotto. If you want to show off, make your own stock. Use leftover chicken with bones, celery, onion, carrots, parsley, pepper corns, and bay leaves. Let simmer for at least an hour, and strain.

Risotto Rice!
Since risotto rice absorbs fluid better then regular rice, it can be stirred longer and therefore releases more starch, which gives the risotto its nice creamy texture. The most famous and popular risotto rices are from Italy, like Arborio or Carnaroli. They are easy to cook al dente which means that they are still a little hard when done.

TARRAGON CHICKEN WITH ANCHOVY CREAM

Serves 4 guests

12 oz, about 2 boneless
    chicken breasts
2 tbsp chopped tarragon
2 tbsp lemon juice
1 tbsp olive oil
Salt and pepper to taste
4 chopsticks, lacquered for
    color

1 tbsp olive oil
2 anchovy fillets in oil
1 tsp lemon zest
2 tbsp lemon juice
½ cup crème fraiche
2 tbsp grated parmesan
    cheese
1 pinch tarragon
Salt and pepper to taste

1. Cut the chicken breast into 1 inch cubes. Place in a Ziplock bag and add the rest of the ingredients. Seal and let marinate in the refrigerator for at least an hour.
2. Turn your oven to broil and skewer the cubes on the chopsticks. If the chopsticks are not lacquered then place them in water for an hour before use, so they won't char in the oven.
3. Grill the skewers in the top of your oven for about 12 minutes or until completely cooked through. Turn after half the time.

Anchovy Cream

1. Heat the olive oil in a small saucepan. Add the anchovy fillets and stir them until they melt.
2. Remove the saucepan from the heat and add the rest of the ingredients. Salt and pepper to taste. Add more lemon juice if you want.

Serving tip!
The skewers can be served both warm and cold.

Simplify:
The sauce tastes better the longer it gets to absorb the flavors, so it can easily be prepared the day before. The same goes for the marinated skewers. Prepare and marinate the day before and just grill before the guests arrive.

For a challenge:
If you have access to a grill, then of course that adds to the flavor. Don't forget to soak nonlacquered skewers beforehand so that they don't catch fire.

LAMB SKEWERS WITH HOT MINT AND PISTACHIO SAUCE

Serves 4 guests

12 oz of tender boneless
    lamb shoulder
2 garlic cloves
3 tbsp lemon juice
Salt and pepper to taste
4 chopsticks, lacquered for
    color

½ cup mint gel
¼ cup pistachio nuts
Cayenne, white and black
Salt and pepper to taste

1. Same preparation as chicken skewers

Hot Mint and Pistachio Sauce

1. Peel and chop the pistachio nuts. Add to a small saucepan and roast for 2 minutes or until hot. Lower the heat and add the mint gel, letting it melt over low heat.
2. Add the peppers to taste. By stirring the peppers, they will cook more evenly.

Serving tip!
You can serve the skewers standing up by skewering them in half a fruit, such as a grapefruit.

Fact!
Lamb that is grain fed has a less gamey flavor than the grass-fed lamb. So if you usually don't like lamb because it is gamey, try grain-fed lamb.

TOMATO AND ARUGULA SALAD WITH BALSAMIC BACON

Serves 4 guests

5 thick slices of bacon
¼ cup of balsamic vinegar
4 tbsp of muscovado sugar
½ pound of cherry tomatoes
½ mango
1 small red onion
¾ pound of arugula
Salt and pepper to taste

1. Cut the bacon slices into 1 inch pieces, and fry it until crispy. To make it crispier and get rid of excess grease, let it sit on a paper towel when done.
2. When the bacon is done, turn off the heat. Carefully add the sugar and then the vinegar to the pan. Watch out for splashes. Salt and pepper to taste.
3. Cut the tomatoes into halves, peel and cut the mango into small cubes, and finely chop the red onion. Add the arugula to your serving bowl. Then add the vinaigrette from the pan and toss well. Finally add the other vegetables and bacon bits.

Simplify:
Prepare the vinaigrette and bacon the day before, and simply heat before serving.

For a challenge:
This dressing works great with a lot of different salad combinations, as long as the base of the salad is arugula or spinach, which can take the heat.

Tip!
In this recipe, bacon fat is used instead of oil in the vinaigrette. If you want a healthier salad, you can drain some of the fat from the pan before mixing the vinaigrette in the pan.

SPICE CRUSTED CHOCOLATE TART WITH PINEAPPLE AND PINK PEPPERCORN COMPOTE

Serves 4 guests

4 tbsp butter
2½ cups of crushed
 graham cracker or
 digestive crackers
 (crumbs)
1½ cups of crushed ginger
 snaps
2 tbsp cacao powder
½ cup sugar

12 oz dark chocolate,
 preferably 60 percent
 cacao content like
 Valhona
7 oz butter
5 egg whites
5 egg yolks
¼ sugar
1¼ heavy cream
3 tbsp cognac (optional)

1. Turn your oven to 425°F. Melt the butter. Crush the crackers and ginger snaps. Mix all the ingredients in a bowl. Add some extra melted butter if the dough gets dry.
2. Using your fingers, press the dough out into a round cake pan 8–10 inches wide. Bake the crust in the middle of the oven for about 15 minutes. When done let the crust cool, and then transfer it to the freezer.

Chocolate Filling

1. Melt the chocolate and butter in the microwave, stirring every 30 seconds until it is a smooth mixture.
2. Let the mixture cool slightly, and then add the egg yokes one at a time while stirring.
3. Beat the egg whites until they create stiff peaks. Add the sugar and beat until hard and white.
4. Carefully stir in the egg-white mixture to the chocolate mixture. Let it cool in the refrigerator.
5. Whip the cream until it is hard, and then add to the chocolate mixture. Add the cognac and return to the refrigerator.
6. Remove the crust from the freezer and add the chocolate filling to the crust. Keep the tart in the fridge until serving.

Serving tip!
It can be messy cutting a mousse tart. Put the knife under hot running water for a smooth and easy cut.

Pineapple and Pink Peppercorn Compote

1 cup pineapple juice
3 tbsp pink peppercorns
4 tbsp sugar
10 oz of fresh pineapple

1. Add the pineapple juice, sugar, and peppercorns in a small sauce pan. Simmer over medium heat for about 20 minutes until the fluid has reduced.
2. Remove the sauce pan from the heat. Chop the pineapple into small cubes and add to the sauce.

Simplify:
Instead of baking the piecrust, you can simply freeze it and add the filling right before serving.

For a challenge:
Individual servings are always great for parties, so use the same recipe but bake in smaller ramekins. Experiment with different flavored compotes. Try peach and liquorish, strawberry and mint, or raspberry and balsamic vinegar.

DINNER

Starts between 6:00 PM and 9:00 PM
A seated dinner is as elegant as a party gets.

MENU

Shrimp Cocktail

–

Ravioli with Smoked Salmon, Spinach, and Lemon

Whiskey Marinated Pork Tenderloin with
Mulligan Spiced Sweet Potatoes

–

Rhubarb and Pear Pie with Gorgonzola

WHAT WE TODAY *consider festive food originated as Grande Cuisine in 18th-century France. Hosts loved to show off their prestige and class, and Grande Cuisine was the ultimate symbol of wealth. It was a sport to make cooking as long and complicated as possible, and a single dinner could consist of over a dozen dishes, expensive ingredients, and loads of exotic spices. Since spices were imported from abroad, they were extremely expensive. The more used in a dish, the more luxurious it was considered to be, with no thought to the flavor or taste. After the French revolution in 1789 and subsequent fall of the aristocrats, dishes were simplified and became accessible to everyone. The new cuisine was dubbed Cuisine Classique and was spearheaded by Auguste Escoffier, the father of modern cooking. Today's style of cooking is called Nouvelle Cuisine, and shies away from overpowering food with lots of spices and sauces. Instead, it focuses on enhancing ingredients' natural flavors.*

DÉCOR

When hosting a dinner, focus on designing a great table. After all, you and your guests will be spending a few hours there, and it is often all the décor you need. A nicely set table looks inviting and enhances the dinner experience by stimulating all the senses. In the chapter "Table Setting" (p. 51-63), you'll find tips, ideas, and guidelines for how to set your dinner table. Use it as an inspiration when planning your table design.

FOOD

The first step in creating a great menu is to utilize ingredients that are in season. Not only do they have the best flavor, but it also keeps your budget down. Put your old food magazines and cookbooks to use when searching for ideas for your menu.

Let the recipes inspire you, and be creative. Pick your favorite sauce from one magazine and the stuffed chicken breast from another. Always simplify the preparation as much as possible when composing party menus to avoid stress. When you've decided on your menu, write it down and make sure your courses work well together. The key is to vary different flavors, but still manage to match them as a whole. Colors should also be taken into consideration; colorful dishes stimulate the senses. Make sure your courses have diverse textures. For example, if you are serving a pork tenderloin with a cream sauce, maybe you should reconsider serving a creamy soup as well. Why not go for a tomato-based soup instead? Don't forget to incorporate your party's theme. When it's time to hit the grocery store, divide your shopping list into different columns for meat, fish, dairy, produce, and dry goods. This will save you time, and keep you from running back and forth from section to section. Bring a calculator so you can easily calculate quantities, and double-check how many containers you might need of a certain ingredient. Prepare as much of the food as possible the day before the party.

SERVICE

If you aim to be a perfect hostess there are a few guidelines to stick to when you are serving your guests. Most etiquette rules are common sense and originated for practical reasons.

- Guest of Honor

The lady seated to the right of the host is the guest of honor and should be served each course first. Continue service counterclockwise, ending with the host.

- Enjoy!

When hot food is served at a table with more than eight people, the guests are welcome to dig in as soon they've been served. If not, they should wait until everyone at the table has been served their food.

- To the left

Plated food is served from the left of the guest, starting with the guest of honor and ending with the host.

- To the right

Beverages are served from the right, and dirty dishes are removed this way as well.

DRINKS

Dinner is commonly accompanied by wine. When serving wine you should also serve water, without ice, since it freezes the taste buds and makes them less sensitive to flavors. Pair the smoked salmon appetizer in this chapter with a robust white or light red wine, and serve a spicy red wine with the flavorful main course. For dessert, a sweet white wine (like ice wine) is recommended. A brave hostess can experiment by pairing teas with her dinner instead.

A Short Wine Guide

Temperature.
In general, we serve our white wines too cold, and our reds too warm. 45°F to 55°F is the right temperature range to serve a white wine, as well as champagne and sparkling wine. If you happen to have a lower quality white wine, serve it colder to mask its taste. Red wines are preferably served at 50°F and 60°F. Red wine has heavier molecules than white and therefore requires a higher temperature for the bouquet to blossom. The theory of room temperature reds is incorrect since it actually refers to temperatures in wine cellars.

Wine and food pairing?
Traditionally white wine is served with lighter and milder foods like vegetarian dishes, fish, chicken, seafood, and turkey. Red wine accompanies dishes with heavier and stronger flavors such as grilled fatty fish, goose, duck, pork, lamb, and beef. However, taste is subjective and these are just guidelines. Today, people experiment more often with wine, and so should you. Give the chardonnay a rest, and try a light red with that fish dish instead.

Quantity?
Etiquette dictates you fill a wine glass no more than three quarters of the way. You may want to serve even less white wine so it stays cool as your guest finishes the glass.

Keep a Party Diary

A hostess on top of her game keeps a party-book where she logs guest lists, menus, recipes, decorations, themes etc. This way she will avoid party faux pas, such as serving her favorite seafood skewer three times in a row to the same guest.

Seasonal Foods

Spring:
asparagus, artichokes, apricots, avocado, carrots, mango, new potatoes, strawberry, spinach

Summer:
beets, blackberries, blueberries, broccoli, corn, cucumbers, nectarines, tomatoes, peaches, plums, zucchini

Fall:
cauliflower, apples, figs, garlic, ginger, grapes, mushrooms, parsnips, sweet potatoes, pomegranate, pears, pumpkins

Winter:
grapefruit, kale, lemons, oranges, radishes, turnips

Food Allergies

Ask guests to RSVP with possible food allergies and vegetarian preferences.

Three Courses for the Stressed-Out Host

Home-cooked meals are always greatly appreciated, especially in today's take-out society. If you really detest cooking or are short on time, but don't want to skimp on that homemade feel, a great compromise is to make an easy appetizer and dessert, and order out for the main course. Hide the take-out carton, and no one will be the wiser.

SHRIMP COCKTAIL

The latest mixology trend is less sweet drinks and a return to those that use bitters. These types of drinks work well before a dinner. With a tomato juice base, this simple drink is garnished with a shrimp to create a true "shrimp cocktail."

1 part lemon vodka
1 part tomato juice
1 large caper berry
1 cooked shrimp

1. Pour equal parts vodka and tomato juice in a large glass or cocktail shaker filled with ice. Shake well.
2. Strain the cocktail, and pour the mixture into a cocktail glass.
3. Garnish with a cooked shrimp on the side of the glass, and place a caper berry in the bottom.

RAVIOLI WITH SMOKED SALMON, SPINACH, AND LEMON

Serves 4 guests

2 oz smoked salmon
2 tbsp ricotta cheese
1 tbsp chopped spinach
4 lasagna plates
1 egg
1 large tomato
Salt and pepper to taste

½ cup heavy cream
½ cup whole milk
1 tsp lemon zest
1 cup grated strong-
    flavored cheese, such
    as parmesan or aged
    gouda
¼ cup smoked almonds
    for garnish
White pepper

1. Finely chop the salmon and mix it with the ricotta cheese and spinach. Pepper to taste, and put the mixture in the refrigerator.
2. Cook the lasagna plates by following the instructions on the package, but cook them to ¾ of the time. Place them directly in an ice bath to cool.
3. Turn your oven to 350°F.
4. Dry the lasagna plates well, and cut them in half. Beat the egg with a fork, and then brush the lasagna plates' edges with the egg mixture.
5. Add one spoonful of the salmon/cheese mixture in the middle of a lasagna plate, add another plate on top, and press the edges together to create a ravioli. Repeat the procedure for the remaining lasagna plates.
6. Cut the tomato into ½ inch thick rounds, salt and pepper. Heat a pan and grill the tomato slices until they get slightly soft.
7. Place the tomato slices on a sheet pan, add one ravioli on each slice. Heat the ravioli in the oven for 5–7 minutes until they are heated completely through.

Cheese Sauce

1. Mix all the ingredients, except the cheese, in a small sauce pan. Bring it to a boil.
2. Lower the heat and add the cheese. Melt the cheese over low heat without letting the mixture boil.
3. Place the tomato slices and ravioli on the serving plates and pour the cheese sauce on top. Chop the smoked almonds and garnish with them.

Simplify:
Both the cheese sauce and the ravioli can be prepared the day before and heated up before serving. The raviolis can also be frozen.

For a challenge:
Add fresh herbs to the sauce for a fresh flavor boost. Try other fillings for the ravioli like shrimp, arugula, or other fish.

WHISKEY MARINATED PORK TENDERLOIN WITH MULLIGAN SPICED SWEET POTATO

Serves 4 guests

1½ pounds of pork
tenderloin
¼ cup honey
¼ cup whiskey
2 tbsp grated ginger
2 tsp cayenne pepper
White and black pepper
Salt to taste

1. Add all the ingredients, except the pork tenderloin, to a bowl. Keep in mind that cayenne pepper can vary in strength, so add a little at a time to taste. Mix the ingredients well, and pour into a large ziplock bag.
2. Add the pork to the bag. Let pork marinate for at least 1 hour in the refrigerator.
3. Remove the tenderloin from the bag, but keep the leftover marinade.
4. Turn your oven to 400°F.
5. Heat a large frying pan and sear the fillet on all sides so it gets an even color. Place the fillet in an oven-safe pan, and cook in the oven for 12–15 minutes depending on how well done you prefer your meat. Pork tenderloin can be served lightly pink in the middle.
6. Remove the tenderloin from the oven and wrap it in foil. Let it sit in the foil for at least 10 minutes. This makes the meat juicier.

Tip!
Fresh ginger is great in marinades and works to tenderize meat. It can be a pain to buy fresh, and it usually ends up rotting in the refrigerator, so keep it in the freezer in a plastic bag instead. When a recipe calls for ginger, just take it out, grate as much as you need, and pop it back in the freezer.

Honey and Whiskey Sauce

Marinade
¼ vegetable bullion cube
1 cup heavy cream
Pepper

1. Pour the leftover marinade into a small saucepan and bring it to a boil. Add the bullion cube, and let the mixture simmer for 5 minutes over medium heat.
2. Lower the heat and add the cream. Pepper to taste.

Mulligan Spiced Sweet Potatoes

4 large sweet potatoes
2 tbsp butter
1 tbsp grated cloves
1 tbsp grated nutmeg
Salt and pepper to taste

1. Turn your oven to 400°F. Peel and cut the potatoes into ¼ inch thick rounds.
2. Place the rounds in a pot filled with cold salted water. Bring it to a boil and then directly remove the potatoes from the heat and strain the water off.
3. Add the butter and spices to the potatoes. Stir until butter melts and the spices are mixed well. Salt and pepper to taste.
4. Place the rounds on a sheet pan, and bake in the oven for about 15 minutes or until the potatoes are soft with a light color.

Brussels Sprouts and Mushroom Compote

10 fresh cremini mush-
rooms
20 fresh Brussels
sprouts
1 yellow onion
3 tbsp butter
¼ cup white wine
Salt and pepper to taste

1. Clean and slice the mushrooms. Clean and cut the Brussels sprouts in half. Peel and chop the onion.
2. Heat up a large frying pan, and melt 1 tbsp of the butter. Add the Brussels sprouts, and sauté quickly at high heat. Add the mushrooms and sauté for about 2 minutes until they have a light golden color. Then add the onion.
3. When all the ingredients have a golden color, add the wine. Lower the heat and let it simmer under a lid.
4. Once most of the fluid is reduced, add the rest of the butter, salt, and pepper to taste. Serve the compote directly.

Simplify:
You can replace sweet potatoes with regular potatoes. Add 2 tablespoons sugar to the spice mix.

For a challenge:
Replace the cremini mushrooms with wild mushrooms, such as chanterelles or whatever is in season.

RHUBARB AND PEAR PIE WITH GORGONZOLA

Pie Crust

Serves 4 guests

4 oz butter
1 ¼ cup flower

1. Cut the butter into small pieces in a bowl. Add the flour and knead quickly into a dough—the less kneading the better. Add the ice-cold water, 1 tbsp at a time, until the dough has a smooth consistency.
2. Let the dough rest in the refrigerator for at least 20 minutes. On a floured work bench, roll the dough out until it's about ¼ inch thick.
3. Turn your oven to 400°F. Fill muffin-tin-sized ramekins with the dough. Press the sides to the tin with a claw or fork. Bake in the middle of the oven for 15 minutes.
4. Once baked, let them cool, and then remove from the tins.

Rhubarb and Pear Filling

½ cup of chopped rhubarb
1 large pear
3 tbsp sugar
2 tbsp lemon juice
2 tbsp sage

1. Clean and chop the rhubarb, and cut the pear into ¼ inch pieces.
2. Place the fruit in a small saucepan, and add the sugar and lemon juice. Simmer at low heat for 15 minutes, or until the rhubarb has melted.
3. Remove the saucepan from the heat and chop and add the sage. Let the filling cool.

Topping

4 oz gorgonzola or other blue vein cheese
6 oz or 4 scoops of lemon sorbet
Lemon zest
Sage leaves

1. Fill the dough shells with the rhubarb and pear filling.
2. Serve on a plate with a slice of blue cheese, a sorbet scoop, and sage leaf and lemon zest for garnish.

Simplify:
Buy ready-made pie shells.

For a challenge:
Serve the pie with different types of blue cheese, like a small cheese plate. Choose cheeses from different countries (for example Roquefort from France, Stilton from England, and Gorgonzola from Italy) and experience the different flavor variations.

Acknowledgments

Thank you to my family, co-workers, and friends for all your inspiration and support throughout this project. To Ingela Holm, for believing in the idea, my wonderful mother who always knew I would write a cookbook, and Robert Andersson, my amazing writer who despite my dyslexia created a great text.

Special thanks to:

– Mezz at Sunwest Studios for having the best-looking photo studio in NYC.
– Anne McDermont and everyone at Party Rental.
– ABC Carpet, for their inspiration and generosity.
– Bodum for always lending us great props.
– Urban Outfitters for fun and inspirational china.
– Whole Foods for having the best grocery store in town.
– Everyone at NYC Flower Market, for putting up with us taking pictures time and time again, especially Fischer Page and G Page.
– Ruth Fischl
– Alex Gomez and everyone at Warwick International Hotels.
– Robert Carroll for all his help.
– Madeleine Werner and Maddesign
– Michael Malmborg and Lyx.
– Kenneth Andersson for his wonderful clothes.

Thank you to all my models for your patience and great appetite: Jay, Oscar, Brad, Helena, Mike, Patrick, Caroline, Camilla, Jesse, Tess, Chad, Rob, Mischa, Dora, and Lucia—you're the best!